ERRATA
The last two plants on page 164 should be
at the beginning of page 165

THE PLANTER'S GUIDE

Barrie Tyler

Phoenix Publishing Associates Ltd.
Bushey, Herts.

First published in Great Britain by

PHOENIX PUBLISHING ASSOCIATES LTD.,
14 Vernon Road, Bushey Herts. WD2 2JL

ISBN 0 9465 7655 6

Printed in Great Britain by
The Garden City Press Limited, Letchworth, Herts
Cover Illustration by Anne Forrest
Cover design by Ivor Claydon
Line Illustrations by Anne Forrest
Typesetting by First Page Ltd., Watford
Database information by Lux Computer Services, Watford

CONTENTS

FOREWORD

The contents of this book have been taken from an extensive plant information system which was invented and designed by the author and installed on computer, at his garden centre in St. Albans, Hertfordshire.

Using this unique system the information built up over several years is now available to gardeners in a clear and usable fashion.

No other gardening book has been written with so much experience as to what garden planters need. Information has been sought from over 250,000 gardeners who have used the data-plant system and from this research the author has been able to establish gardeners priorities, likes and dislikes, and reasons for past successes and failures.

The key priority from the research is the need for information on plants by height; then by soil and prevailing light conditions.

The list of Shrubs, Conifers, Heathers and Climbing Plants shown in this book is given under the priorities and is available from medium and large garden centres. This guide is designed to help you choose the correct plants for your garden and can be used in conjunction with other publications for pruning, pollination and general care.

INTRODUCTION

This book is divided into three sections for ease of use and quick reference based on gardeners needs which we found during our research.

1. Plants by Height, Type, Deciduous or Evergreen, Moisture Level, Light, Soil type, Position and Best Month of Display

2. Full description of all plants found in the book

3. A Botanical to Common; Common to Botanical name list

Decide on the height of plants wanted to enhance your garden. Then check the soil, position, light, moisture and best month of flowering or display you want. Choose whether or not you want deciduous or evergreen shrubs and then marry up your list of requirements with the grid of plants given under the five height scales.

Remember that a prime consideration will be the eventual full height of the plant as this will effect the overall appearance of your garden more than anything else. When you have found a list of likely plants which suit your conditions then turn to the second part of the book for a full description of the plants you have chosen. To help you further we have given an explanation of our definition of moisture level, light, position and soil conditions.

We recommend that you read these notes as there are many misunderstandings over the definition of conditions such as position.

It is a good idea to draw a sketch plan of your border/bed to be planted and to write in the chosen shrubs and conifers to give you an idea in your mind's eye of the eventual colour of flower and foliage. To help you with your planning we have given a couple of examples of bed planning at the end of our opening section. We recommend that you take this book with you when visiting garden centres as a handy reference aid and, besides, it will save you having to ask questions.

Acknowledgement

Our special thanks go to John B. Westacott for his time and horticultural experience in checking the database information for the Data-Plant computer system from which the contents of this book have been taken.

Barrie Tyler
Burston-Tyler Rose and Garden Centre Ltd.
Chiswell Green, St. Albans, Herts.

HEIGHT

Height figures and indicators given in this book are shown in feet and inches as we still find this the most readily understood by gardeners.

The height of a plant is given either as the 10 year height of growth or, if the plant reaches maturity before 10 years, its anticipated final height under average growing conditions.

Bear in mind that extreme climatic and soil conditions will effect the height of all plants.

With climbing plants, if the height is given as 15 feet then, if the plant is running vertically for 5 feet, it will travel up to 10 feet horizontally. Often plants will flower better on horizontal growth.

When planting a border adjacent to a fence or wall it is better to choose plants which grow slightly taller than the backdrop as this will ensure that the skyline is broken and softened by the plants. Having chosen the backdrop you can then choose your foreground plants by height and colour allowing for the other conditions in the bed.

DECIDUOUS OR EVERGREEN?

The choice must be yours as too many evergreens can make your garden look very dull or 'heavy', particularly during winter months.

Many deciduous plants, but only a few evergreens, have beautiful autumn tints and will give a longer life to your garden from a colour point of view.

NB Some evergreens will lose some of their leaves during severe winters and are therefore referred to as 'semi-evergreen' in the plant description part of the book.

Remember also that as evergreens mature they will shed some of their older leaves usually as new growth commences.

MOISTURE LEVELS

Soils are very complex in their structures; some retaining moisture, some free draining and other with excessive amounts of sticky clay which is cold and wet in winter and bakes hard in summer.

Most plants will tolerate all these conditions but some will do better than others so put the most suitable plants in these areas as indicated in the site column.

Beware of waterlogged sites which flood in winter and still retain water under the surface in the summer.

Take professional advice on how to drain a heavily waterlogged area as there are few plants that will live in these conditions.

If you have dry conditions that are adverse to the plant you particularly want to grow you can help considerably by incorporating moisture retaining material such as peat, compost or well rotted manure in the spit of soil below and surrounding the root ball of the plant.

For wet sites you can incorporate river washed sharp sand and other gritty material in the spit below the root area before planting.

Heavy clay soils are a problem and are often treated incorrectly by most gardeners who are over anxious to dig in vast quantities of humus. It is doubtful if this action will improve the soil to any great extent for many years. Forget the digging and just shape up the bed in question, and remove the perennial weeds physically or chemically.

This is easiest to do in the spring when the soil is starting to dry and the weeds are growing quickly and are at their most susceptible to weedlillers.

Make a good job of preparing each planting hole in accordance with the planting instructions contained later in this book. With the planting complete, top dress the whole of the bed with moss peat, or compost, to a depth of one or two inches and never dig again. Hoe to kill off any weeds. Nature, and the hoe, will take the peat into the top two or three inches of clay and within a year or two the surface will be fine and friable, the weeds will pull out easily and the plants will be very healthy. Top dress with peat *at least* once a year.

Be careful when hoeing near surface rooting plants such as heathers and rhododendrons.

Remember when we indicate in the tables that a plant will stand dry conditions we mean *after* it is established. You cannot really expect to take a plant home and drop it into sand and expect it to flourish!

A = Any

N = Normal well drained soil

D = Normal to dry

W = Normal to wet

LIGHT

It is easy to determine the light condition in your garden by observing the area to be planted in the early morning, mid-day and evening.

If, for the greater part of the day, and particularly the early afternoon, the area in question is in sun then it is sufficient to mark your plan as 'full sun'.

Part sun will be either all of the morning or the bulk of the afternoon sun. Dappled light through trees should be regarded as semi shade.

F = Full sun

FP = Full sun/Partial shade

S = Shade/Partial Shade

A = Any

SOIL TYPE

Acid, Alkaline or Normal?

Not everyone knows the ph value of their soil which can vary from place to place in the garden. It is very obvious in some areas of a garden what the soil condition are by large deposits of chalk(indicating lime conditions) or whether or not your near neighbours are growing lime hating plants such as Rhododendrons and Azaleas.

It is important to know if your soil is on the extremes of the PH scale. Some garden centres will test a sample of your soil for you which would be worth any nominal charge if you are keen to grow some of the more expensive limehaters.

The ideal PH is in the range 6.4 to 6.8 (PH 7 is neutral)

Remember it is relatively easy to make your soil alkaline by dressing it with lime but do this only if it is really necessary as it is an exceedingly slow process to reverse. Fortunately nature will slowly reduce the degree of alkalinity in cultivated soil and you can help it by adding humus to the soil in the form of leaf mould, compost or peat.

You can also cheat nature to some extent, if the soil is not too alkaline, by planting lime hating plants in generous amounts of peat mixed in with the soil, and then top dressing with peat over the root area each year. Bear in mind that peat has little or no nutritional value although it is an excellent soil conditioner.

A = Acid

C = Chalky

N = Neutral

POSITION

Position, in the context of this book, refers to exposure to excessive amounts of winds which can be damaging to plants.

Not only do cold winds affect plants but excessively warm winds can increase the plants' transpiration over and above the ability of its stems and root system to supply moisture to the tips of the leaves quickly enough to replace the evaporated moisture.

Protection, by netting, until a plant is established may be the answer to growing a tender shrub in an over windy place. Most fenced off hedged gardens would be regarded as sheltered areas but beware, for example, of the wind funneling between two houses as this can be very damaging to the first plants it meets.

Plant shrubs suitable for exposed areas and then more tender plants on the leeward side of the growing wind break.

Gardens most definitely do have climatic regions.

S = **Sheltered**

E = **Exposed**

A = **Average**

BEST MONTHS OF DISPLAY

Many of the plants listed in this book have more than one 'best period' of display.

For example Pyracantha has an attractive flower in the spring but many gardeners prefer it for its rich red berries in the autumn.

Where possible we have attempted to show both periods where we feel that the plant truly has two 'best periods' of display. In other cases we have taken what we feel to be the best month of display which in some cases may be the flower, in others the berry or the foliage.

You may disagree with us in our feelings on the best month but then, at the end of the day, you are choosing the plants for your garden to look at their best when you want them too.

PLANT INDEX

All plants have botanical names which are often lengthy or tongue twisters and, as a consequence, popular names have evolved for many plants. Some plants have several common names or conversely, one common name may apply to more than one type of plant. At the back of the book there is a cross reference to botanical to common and, where available, common to botanical. Both lists are in alphabetical order.

Although not strictly correct botanically, we have listed Azalea under A for ease of identity by the majority of gardeners. They are 'correctly' Rhododendron.

Furthermore the evergreen cultivars are all included as A.Japonica or Japanese Azalea which most of them are not being cultivars raised in Holland, United Kingdom and the United States of America.

One other botanical anomaly is that bipeneric hybrids such as Osmaria and Stranviria are not prefixed by X as they should be.

We trust that these small adjustments do not interfere with your overall enjoyment of the indexing section.

PLANTING

A lot of time and, often, a lot of money, is spent on acquiring plants but too little thought and effort go into planting.

A well prepared planting hole is essential. A stout stake and a proper 'tie' (not string) will get a tall shrub or tree off to a good start. The careful use of secateurs to prune or tidy a plant is often necessary.

Food in the growing season gives a plant vitality and sensible watering is crucial to any plant's survival.

When planting in lawn areas always remove the turf from at least two feet around the stem of the plant. If the turf is left to smother the plant it will not grow, althought it may survive in a stunted form. Once the plant is well established, after four or five years, the turf may be replaced.

Plants purchased today are, by and large, 'container grown' which enables gardeners to plant virtually year round. However, as the root system of the plant has been restricted in its container it may well have a very dense root ball. As a consequence any water applied will be inclined to run around the root ball into the newly dug soil of the planting hole leaving the roots dry. A soaking one or twice a week, slowly applied by hose or can, is better than a daily shower.

Preparing A Planting Hole

Dig a hole twice the depth and twice the width of the container which should then be removed carefully from the plant to be used.

Using the container, mix two fills of moist peat with a handful of bone meal (hoof and horn for limehaters) and some of the soil taken from the planting hole. Place the plant in the same depth as it was in the container. As you do this free some of the lower roots from the ball and spread them out before filling the hole with the remaining mixture.

Firm the soil, using your heel for larger plants, then water well and stake and tie if necessary.

Climbing shrubs, particularly clematis, should be planted 3 inches below soil surface and cut down to 9 inches above the ground regardless of time of year, variety or how much top growth there is on the plant when purchased.

Soil next to a wall or fence is often dry therefore plant 12 inches away, if possible, and lead the plant to the fence or trellis with a bamboo cane which can later be removed once the plant has established itself on the main support.

Do not prepare holes in advance as they can easily fill with rain water and become waterlogged, nor should you plant when the ground is frozen. It does not matter however if the ground freezes immediately after planting as the roots of your plant will be protected.

Garden Design Notes

As a garden can be 'a joy forever' forward planning for flowers, shape, texture of foliage, autumn leaf colour, winter berries and fragrance should be undertaken very carefully.

In this book we have covered the four categories which are easiest to maintain, conifers, heathers, shrubs and climbers, now the rest is up to you.

To help you plan your planting and give you some food for thought we have provided you with a couple of sample beds but we are sure you can add your own touches to include your own favourites.

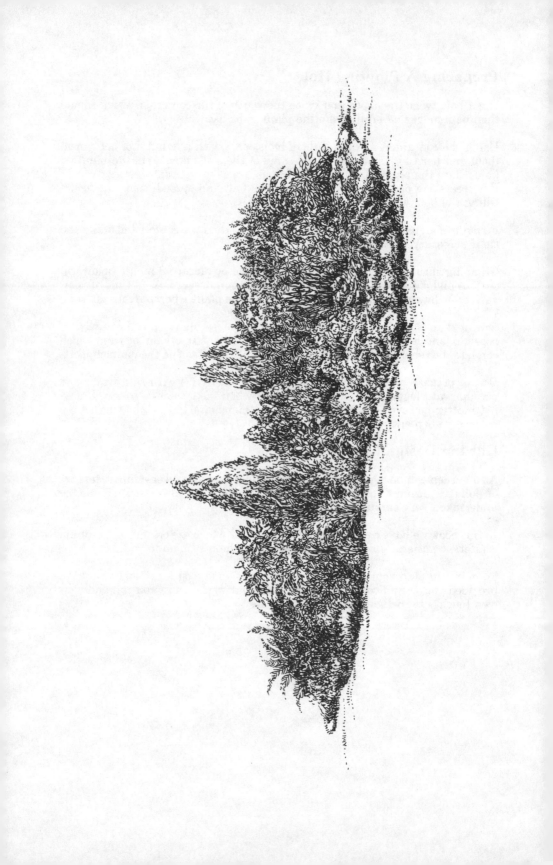

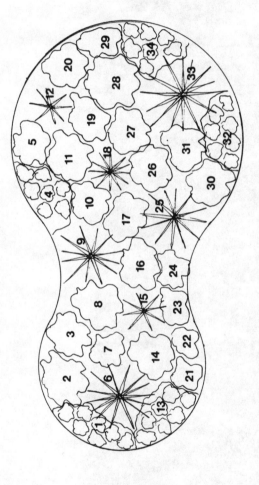

1   ERICA CARNEA 'MYRETOUN RUBY' (x7)
2   CISTUS PURPUREUS
3   HEBE RAKAIENSIS
4   CALLUNA VULGARIS 'ROBERT CHAPMAN' (x7)
5   HEBE ALBICANS
6   JUNIPERUS X MEDIA 'OLD GOLD'
7   CARYOPTERIS X CLANDONENSIS
8   SPIRAEA JAPONICA 'GOLDEN PRINCESS'
9   CHAMAECYPARIS OBTUSA 'NANA GRACILIS'
10 CERATOSTIGMA WILMOTTIANUM
11 CYTISUS PRAECOX
12 JUNIPERUS SQUAMATA 'BLUE STAR'
13 CALLUNA VULGARIS 'H.E. BEALE' (x7)
14 CYTISUS PRAECOX 'ALL GOLD'
15 JUNIPERUS CHINENSIS
16 MYRTUS APICULATA
17 DAPHNE MEZEREUM 'GLEN GLEAM'

18 CHAMAECYPARIS LAWSONIANA 'ELLWOOD'S GOLD'
19 SPIRAEA JAPONICA 'LITTLE PRINCESS'
20 BERBERIS THUNBERGII ATROPURPUREA NANA
21 HEBE PINGUIFOLIA 'PAGEI'
22 FUCHSIA 'TOM THUMB'
23 PHORMIUM TENAX 'BRONZE BABY'
24 GENISTA LYDIA
25 THUJA OCCIDENTALIS 'DANICA'
26 POTENTILLA FRUTICOSA
27 PHORMIUM TENAX 'YELLOW WAVE'
28 ABELIA X GRANDIFLORA
29 HEBE 'JAMES STIRLING'
30 BERBERIS BUXIFOLIA 'NANA'
31 CISTUS 'SUNSET'
32 CALLUNA VULGARIS 'DRUM-RA' (x7)
33 JUNIPERUS SQUAMATA 'BLUE CARPET'
34 ERICA X DARLEYENSIS 'SILBERSCHMELZE' (x7)

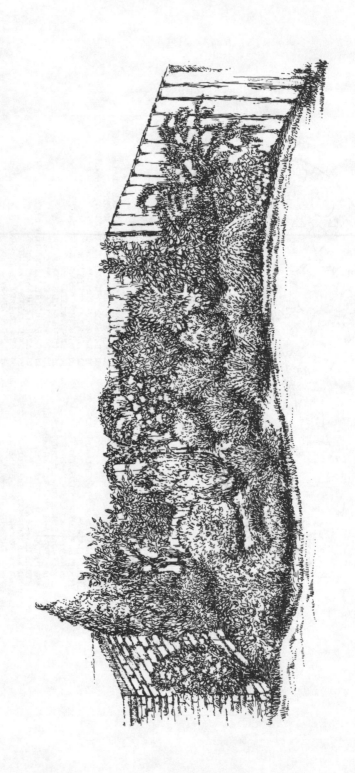

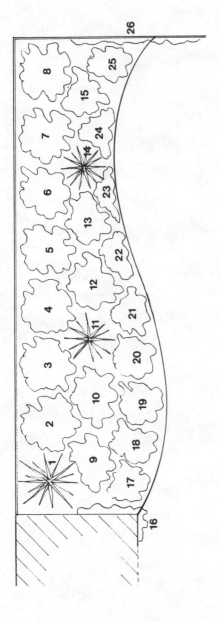

1. THUJA PLICATA
2. CORNUS ALBA 'ELEGANTISSIMA'
3. RHODODENDRON 'PINK PEARL'
4. PHILADELPHUS 'VIRGINAL'
5. CAMELLIA X WILLIAMSII 'DONATION'
6. SKIMMIA JAPONICA 'FOREMANII'
7. WEIGELA 'NEWPORT RED'
8. VIBURNUM BURKWOODII
9. FATSIA JAPONICA
10. SKIMMIA JAPONICA 'RUBELLA'
11. CHAMAECYPARIS LAWSONIANA 'ELLWOODII'
12. X OSMAREA BURKWOODII
13. FUCHSIA MAGELLANICA 'VARIEGATA'

14. CHAMAECYPARIS OBTUSA 'NANA GRACILIS'
15. CHOISYA TERNATA
16. CHAENOMELES SPECIOSA 'SARGENTII'
17. VIBURNUM DAVIDII
18. FUCHSIA 'MME CORNELISSEN'
19. ERICA DARLEYENSIS 'SILBERSCHMELZE'
20. EUONYMUS FORTUNEI 'EMERALD 'N GOLD'
21. SARCOCOCCA HUMILIS
22. ERICA CARNEA 'MYRETOUN RUBY'
23. EUONYMUS FORTUNEI 'EMERALD GAIETY'
24. BERBERIS THUNBERGII 'AUREA'
25. RHODODENDRON 'CARMEN'
26. COTONEASTER HORIZONTALIS

Shrubs, Conifers and Heathers
to a Height of One Foot

Height up to 1 ft.

		TYPE	DECIDUOUS/EVERGREEN	MOISTURE LEVEL	LIGHT	SOIL	POSITION	BEST MONTH
Andromeda polifolia	Compacta	S	E	W	S	A	A	5-6
Calluna vulgaris	Alba Plena	H	E	A	F	A	E	8-9
	Alba Rigida	H	E	A	F	A	E	7-9
	County Wicklow	H	E	A	F	A	E	8-9
	Golden Carpet	H	E	A	F	A	E	8-9
	Golden Feather	H	E	A	F	A	E	8-10
	J.H. Hamilton	H	E	A	F	A	E	8-9
	John F. Letts	H	E	A	F	A	E	8-9
	Kinlochruel	H	E	A	F	A	E	8-9
	Multicolor	H	E	A	F	A	E	8-9
	Orange Queen	H	E	A	F	A	E	8-9
	Robert Chapman	H	E	A	F	A	E	8-9
	Ruth Sparkes	H	E	A	F	A	E	8-9
	Sir John Charrington	H	E	A	F	A	E	8-9
	Sister Anne	H	E	A	F	A	E	8-9
	White Lawn	H	E	A	F	A	E	8-10
	Winter Chocolate	H	E	A	F	A	E	8-9
Ceratostigma griffithii		S	E	N	F	N	S	8-10
Chamaecyparis lawsoniana	Gnome	C	E	N	A	N	A	1-12
	Pygmaea Argentea	C	E	N	FP	N	A	1-12
Chamaecyparis pisifera	Nana Aureovariegata	C	E	N	FP	N	A	1-12
	Nana	C	E	N	A	N	A	1-12
Cornus canadensis		S	D	A	S	A	A	4-11
Cotoneaster congestus		S	E	N	FP	N	A	11-12

Height up to 1 ft.

		TYPE	DECIDUOUS/EVERGREEN	MOISTURE LEVEL	LIGHT	SOIL	POSITION	BEST MONTH
Cotoneaster congestus	Nanus	S	E	A	FP	N	A	10-12
Cotoneaster dammeri	Coral Beauty	S	E	N	A	N	A	11-12
Cryptomeria japonica	Vilmoriniana	C	E	W	FP	N	A	1-12
Daphne cneorum		S	E	N	FP	N	S	5-6
Erica carnea		H	E	A	FP	N	E	1-4
Erica carnea	Ada Collins	H	E	A	FP	N	E	3-4
	Ann Sparkes	H	E	A	FP	N	E	12-3
	Aurea	H	E	A	FP	N	E	12-3
	December Red	H	E	A	FP	N	E	1-2
	Foxhollow	H	E	A	FP	N	E	2-4
	Heathwood	H	E	A	FP	N	E	2-4
	James Backhouse	H	E	A	FP	N	E	1-3
	King George	H	E	A	FP	N	E	12-4
	Loughrigg	H	E	A	FP	N	E	2-3
	Myretoun Ruby	H	E	A	FP	N	E	2-4
	Pink Spangles	H	E	A	FP	N	E	3-4
	Praecox Rubra	H	E	A	FP	N	E	1-3
	Prince of Wales	H	E	A	FP	N	E	3-4
	Ruby Glow	H	E	A	FP	N	E	1-3
	Springwood Pink	H	E	A	FP	N	E	1-3
	Springwood White	H	E	A	FP	N	E	1-3
	Vivellii	H	E	A	FP	N	E	1-3
	Winter Beauty	H	E	A	FP	N	E	1-2
Erica cinerea	Alba Minor	H	E	A	F	A	E	6-10

		TYPE	DECIDUOUS/EVERGREEN	MOISTURE LEVEL	LIGHT	SOIL	POSITION	BEST MONTH
Erica cinerea	Atrosanguinea	H	E	A	F	A	E	6-8
	C.D. Eason	H	E	A	F	A	E	6-9
	Contrast	H	E	A	F	A	E	6-8
	Pink Foam	H	E	A	F	A	E	6-9
	Pink Ice	H	E	A	F	A	E	6-9
	Stephen Davis	H	E	A	F	A	E	6-8
	Velvet Night	H	E	A	F	A	E	6-8
Erica tetralix	Alba Mollis	H	E	A	F	A	E	6-10
	Con Underwood	H	E	A	F	A	E	6-10
Erica vagans	Mrs D.F. Maxwell	H	E	A	FP	A	E	8-10
	St. Keverne	H	E	A	FP	A	E	8-9
	Valerie Proudley	H	E	A	FP	A	E	8-9
Erica x watsonii	Dawn	H	E	A	FP	A	E	7-9
Euonymus fortunei	Sun Spot	S	E	A	A	N	E	1-12
Gaultheria procumbens		S	E	A	A	A	E	9-2
Genista pilosa		S	D	D	F	N	E	6
Hebe	Carl Teschner	S	E	N	FP	N	A	6-7
Hebe ochracea	James Stirling	S	E	N	F	N	A	1-12
Hedera canariensis	Variegata	S	E	A	A	N	A	1-12
Hedera colchica	Dentata Variegata	S	E	A	A	N	A	1-12
	Paddy's Pride (Sulphur Heart)	S	E	A	A	N	A	1-12
Hedera helix	Anna Marie	S	E	A	A	N	A	1-12
	Boskoop	S	E	A	A	N	A	1-12

Height up to 1 ft.

		BEST MONTH	POSITION	SOIL	LIGHT	MOISTURE LEVEL	DECIDUOUS/EVERGREEN	TYPE
Hedera helix	Cavendishii	S	E	A	A	N	A	1-12
	Cristata	S	E	A	A	N	A	1-12
	Deltoidea	S	E	A	A	N	A	1-12
	Gavotte	S	E	A	A	N	A	1-12
	Glacier	S	E	A	A	N	A	1-12
	Goldheart	S	E	A	A	N	A	1-12
	Green Ripple	S	E	A	A	N	A	1-12
	Ivalace	S	E	A	A	N	A	1-12
	Little Picture	S	E	A	A	N	A	1-12
	Lutzii	S	E	A	A	N	A	1-12
	Sagittifolia	S	E	A	A	N	A	1-12
Juniperus communis	Depressa Aurea	C	E	A	F	N	E	4-6
	Green Carpet	C	E	A	A	N	E	1-12
	Repanda	C	E	A	A	N	E	1-12
Juniperus horizontalis	Blue Chip ('Blue Moon')	C	E	A	FP	N	E	1-12
	Emerald Spreader	C	E	A	A	N	E	1-12
	Glauca	C	E	A	F	N	E	1-12
	Hughes	C	E	A	FP	N	E	1-12
Juniperus procumbens	Nana	C	E	A	A	N	E	1-12
Juniperus sabina	Tamariscifolia	C	E	A	A	N	E	1-12
Juniperus squamata	Blue Carpet	C	E	A	FP	N	E	1-12
Juniperus taxifolia	Lutchuensis	C	E	A	FP	N	E	1-12
Microbiota decussata		C	E	A	A	N	E	1-12
Picea abies	Little Gem	C	E	A	FP	N	A	4-6

Height up to 1 ft.

		BEST MONTH	POSITION	SOIL	LIGHT	MOISTURE LEVEL	DECIDUOUS/EVERGREEN	TYPE
Picea mariana	Nana	C	E	A	FP	A	N	1-12
Rhododendron	Pink Drift	S	E	W	FP	A	A	5-6
	Songbird	S	E	W	FP	A	A	4
Rhododendron impeditum		S	E	W	FP	A	A	4-5
Rubus tricolor		S	E	A	A	N	E	7
Thuja plicata	Rogersii	C	E	A	F	N	A	1-12
Vinca minor		S	E	A	A	N	E	4-6
Vinca minor	Atropurpurea	S	E	A	A	N	E	5-7
	Bowles Variety	S	E	A	A	N	E	4-6

Shrubs, Conifers and Heathers
to a Height of Two Foot

Height up to 2 ft.

		BEST MONTH	POSITION	SOIL	LIGHT	MOISTURE LEVEL	DECIDUOUS/EVERGREEN	TYPE
Abies balsamea		C	E	A	A	N	A	4-6
Arundinaria pygmaea		S	E	W	A	N	A	1-12
Azalea japonica	Blue Danube	S	E	W	S	A	A	4-5
	Hatsugiri	S	E	W	S	A	A	4-5
Berberis buxifolia	Nana	S	E	N	F	N	E	10-2
Berberis thunbergii	Atropurpurea Nana	S	D	N	F	N	E	4-10
Calluna vulgaris	Beoley Gold	H	E	A	F	A	E	8-9
	Allegro	H	E	A	F	A	E	8-9
	Alportii	H	E	A	F	A	E	8-9
	Blazeaway	H	E	A	F	A	E	8-9
	Bonfire Brilliance	H	E	A	F	A	E	8-9
	Boskoop	H	E	A	F	A	E	8-9
	Cuprea	H	E	A	F	A	E	8-9
	Darkness	H	E	A	F	A	E	8-9
	Drum-Ra	H	E	A	F	A	E	8-9
	Elsie Purnell	H	E	A	F	A	E	8-9
	Gold Haze	H	E	A	F	A	E	8-9
	H.E. Beale	H	E	A	F	A	E	9-10
	Hammondii	H	E	A	F	A	E	8-9
	Joy Vanstone	H	E	A	F	A	E	8-9
	Peter Sparkes	H	E	A	F	A	E	8-9
	Ralph Purnell	H	E	A	F	A	E	7-9
	Serlei Aurea	H	E	A	F	A	E	8-10
	Silver Queen	H	E	A	F	A	E	8-9

6

Height up to 2 ft.

		BEST MONTH	POSITION	SOIL	LIGHT	MOISTURE LEVEL	DECIDUOUS/EVERGREEN	TYPE
Calluna vulgaris	Silver Rose	H	E	A	F	A	E	8-9
	Sunrise	H	E	A	F	A	E	8-10
	Sunset	H	E	A	F	A	E	8-9
	Underwoodii	H	E	A	F	A	E	8-9
Calluna vulgaris cultivars		H	E	A	F	A	E	8-9
Ceratostigma plumbaginoides		S	D	N	F	N	A	7-10
Chamaecyparis lawsoniana	Minima Aurea	C	E	N	F	N	A	1-12
	Minima Glauca	C	E	N	A	N	A	1-12
Chamaecyparis obtusa	Nana Lutea	C	E	N	F	N	A	1-12
Cryptomeria japonica	Globosa Nana	C	E	N	A	N	A	1-12
Cytisus x kewensis		S	D	D	F	N	E	5
Daboecia cantabrica	Atropurpurea	H	E	A	F	A	E	6-9
	Donards Pink	H	E	A	F	A	A	6-10
Daboecia species & cultivars		H	E	A	F	A	A	6-7
Erica carnea		H	E	A	FP	N	E	1-2
Erica cinerea		H	E	A	F	A	E	7-9
Erica cinerea	Hookstone White	H	E	A	F	A	E	6-8
Erica erigena (mediterranea)	Brightness	H	E	A	FP	N	E	3-5
	W.T.Rackliff	H	E	A	FP	N	E	1-4
Erica vagans		H	E	A	F	A	E	8-10
Erica vagans	Lyonesse	H	E	A	F	A	E	8-10
Erica x darleyensis		H	E	A	FP	N	E	1-3
Erica x darleynsis	Arthur Johnson	H	E	A	FP	N	E	1-3

Height up to 2 ft.

		BEST MONTH	POSITION	SOIL	LIGHT	MOISTURE LEVEL	DECIDUOUS/EVERGREEN	TYPE
Erica x darleynsis	Darley Dale	H	E	A	FP	N	E	12-3
	Furzey	H	E	A	FP	N	E	1-3
	George Rendall	H	E	A	FP	N	E	1-3
	Ghost Hills	H	E	A	FP	N	E	11-3
	Jack H. Brummage	H	E	A	FP	N	E	2-3
	Silberschmelze	H	E	A	A	N	E	1-4
Erica x watsonii		H	E	A	F	A	E	7-9
Euonymus fortunei	Emerald Gaiety	S	E	A	A	N	E	1-12
	Emerald and Gold	S	E	A	A	N	E	1-12
	Sun Spot	S	E	A	A	N	E	1-12
	Variegatus	S	E	A	A	N	E	1-12
Fuchsia	Brilliant	S	D	N	A	N	S	7-10
	Corallina	S	D	N	A	N	S	7-10
	Lady Thumb	S	D	N	A	N	A	6-10
	Lena	S	D	N	A	N	A	6-9
	Margaret Brown	S	D	N	A	N	S	7-10
	Peter Pan	S	D	N	A	N	A	7-10
	Prosperity	S	D	N	A	N	S	6-10
	Tom Thumb	S	D	N	A	N	A	6-9
Genista tinctoria	Plena	S	D	D	F	N	E	6-8
Hebe	White Gem	S	E	D	F	N	A	6-7
Hebe franciscana	Variegata	S	E	D	F	N	S	7-9
Hebe pinquifolia	Pagei	S	E	D	FP	N	A	5
Hebe rakaiensis (subalpina)		S	E	D	F	N	A	6-7

Height up to 2 ft.

		TYPE	DECIDUOUS/EVERGREEN	MOISTURE LEVEL	LIGHT	SOIL	POSITION	BEST MONTH
Hypericum calycinum		S	E	A	A	N	E	7-10
Hypericum moseranum	Tricolor	S	D	N	P	N	A	6-8
Ilex crenata	Golden Gem	S	E	D	FP	N	E	1-12
Juniperus communis	Compressa	C	E	A	A	N	A	1-12
Juniperus conferta		C	E	A	FP	N	A	1-12
Juniperus horizontalis	Plumosa Compacta	C	E	A	A	N	E	1-12
	Plumosa Youngstown	C	E	A	A	N	E	1-12
	Winter Blue	C	E	A	A	N	E	1-12
Juniperus squamata	Blue Star	C	E	A	FP	N	E	1-12
Juniperus virginiana	Silver Spreader	C	E	A	FP	N	E	1-12
Juniperus x davurica	Expansa Aureospicata	C	E	A	FP	N	E	1-12
Juniperus x media	Gold sovereign	C	E	N	F	N	E	1-12
Lavandula	Hidcote	S	E	D	F	N	A	7-9
Nandina domestica	Pygmaea	S	E	A	F	N	S	4-10
Pachysandra terminalis		S	E	A	A	N	E	2-3
Pachysandra terminalis	Variegata	S	E	A	FP	N	E	1-12
Phormium tenax	Bronze Baby	S	E	D	F	N	A	1-12
Picea abies	Nidiformis	C	E	N	A	N	A	1-12
Picea glauca	Alberta Globe	C	E	N	A	N	A	1-12
Picea mariana	Ericoides	C	E	N	F	N	A	1-12
Pinus mugo	Humpy	C	E	N	A	N	A	1-12
	Mops	C	E	N	A	N	A	1-12
	Ophir	C	E	N	F	N	A	1-12
Potentilla arbuscula		S	D	D	FP	N	E	6-9

Height up to 2 ft.

	BEST MONTH POSITION SOIL LIGHT MOISTURE LEVEL DECIDUOUS/EVERGREEN TYPE							
Potentilla dahurica	Abbotswood	S	D	D	FP	N	E	6-10
Potentilla x fruticosa	Princess	S	D	D	FP	N	E	5-8
Rhododendron	Bengal	S	E	W	FP	A	A	5
	Curlew	S	E	W	FP	A	A	5
	Golden Gate	S	E	W	FP	A	A	5
	Moerheim	S	E	W	FP	A	A	4-5
	Sapphire	S	E	W	FP	A	A	5
Rhododendron fastigiatum		S	E	W	FP	A	A	4-5
Rhododendron kiusianum		S	E	W	FP	A	A	5-6
Rhododendron lapponicum	Hillier's Form	S	E	W	FP	A	A	4
Ruta graveolens	Jackman's Blue	S	E	D	F	N	A	5-10
Santolina chamaecyparissus		S	E	D	F	N	A	4-10
Sarcococca humilis		S	E	N	A	N	A	2-3
Spiraea japonica	Alpina	S	E	N	FP	N	A	6-8
	Little Princess	S	D	N	FP	N	A	6-8
	Shirobana	S	D	N	FP	N	A	7-9
Taxus baccata	Summergold	C	E	N	F	N	A	1-12
Thuja occidentalis	Danica	C	E	N	A	N	A	1-12
	Golden Globe	C	E	N	F	N	A	1-12
Tsuga canadensis	Jeddeloh	C	E	N	FP	N	A	1-12

Shrubs, Conifers and Heathers
to a Height of Three Foot

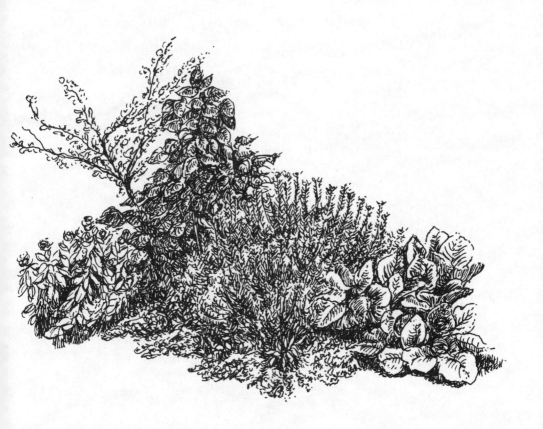

Height up to 3 ft.

		TYPE	DECIDUOUS/EVERGREEN	MOISTURE LEVEL	LIGHT	SOIL	POSITION	BEST MONTH
Abies lasiocarpa	Compacta	C	E	A	FP	N	A	5-7
Abies procera	Glauca Prostrata	C	E	A	F	N	A	1-12
Artemesia absinthium	Lambrook silver	S	E	D	F	N	A	6-10
Azalea japonica	Achgadir	S	E	W	FP	A	A	4-5
	Aladdin	S	E	W	FP	A	A	4-5
	Amoena	S	E	W	FP	A	A	5
	Arendsii	S	E	W	FP	A	A	4-5
	Blaauws Pink	S	E	W	FP	A	A	4-5
	Esmeralda	S	E	W	FP	A	A	4-5
	Excelsior	S	E	W	FP	A	A	4-5
	Favorite	S	E	W	FP	A	A	4-5
	Fedora	S	E	W	FP	A	A	4-5
	Hino Crimson	S	E	W	FP	A	A	4-5
	Ima-Shojo	S	E	W	FP	A	A	5
	Kermissine	S	E	W	FP	A	A	4-5
	Lilli Marlene	S	E	W	FP	A	A	5
	Mikador	S	E	W	FP	A	A	4-5
	Mother's Day	S	E	W	FP	A	A	4-5
	Red Pimpernel	S	E	W	FP	A	A	5-6
	Rose Bud	S	E	W	FP	A	A	5
	Silvester	S	E	W	FP	A	A	4
	Thierry	S	E	W	FP	A	A	4-5
	Vuyk's Rosyred	S	E	W	FP	A	A	4-5
	Vuyk's Scarlet	S	E	W	FP	A	A	4-5

11

Height up to 3 ft.

		TYPE	DECIDUOUS/EVERGREEN	MOISTURE LEVEL	LIGHT	SOIL	POSITION	BEST MONTH
Azalea japonica (General)		S	E	W	FP	A	A	4-5
Berberis Parkjuweel		S	E	N	F	N	A	8-10
Caryopteris x clandonensis		S	D	D	F	N	A	6-9
Caryopteris x clandonensis	Heavenly Blue	S	D	D	F	N	A	8-9
	Kew Blue	S	D	D	F	N	A	8-9
Cedrus deodara	Golden Horizon	C	E	N	F	N	A	3-7
Ceratostigma willmottianum		S	D	N	F	N	A	7-10
Chamaecyparis lawsoniana	Silver Threads	C	E	N	FP	N	A	1-12
Chamaecyparis obtusa	Nana Gracilis	C	E	N	A	N	A	1-12
Chamaecyparis pisifera	Filifera Aurea	C	E	N	FP	N	A	1-12
	Filifera Nana	C	E	A	A	N	A	1-12
	Filifera Sungold	C	E	N	F	N	A	3-9
Chamaecyparis thyoides	Andelyensis	C	E	N	A	N	A	1-12
Cistus	Silver Pink	S	E	D	F	N	A	6-7
Cistus x loretii		S	E	D	F	N	A	6-7
Convolvulus cneorum		S	E	D	F	N	S	6-8
Cytisus x praecox	Allgold	S	D	D	F	N	E	5-6
Erica erigena (mediterranea)		H	E	A	FP	N	E	4
Erica erigena (mediterranea)	Golden Lady	H	E	A	FP	N	E	3-5
Euonymus japonica	Microphyllus Variegatus	S	E	A	P	N	A	1-12
Fuchsia	Alice Hoffman	S	D	N	A	N	A	6-9
	Constance	S	D	N	A	N	A	7-10
	Genii	S	D	N	F	N	A	6-9
	Pixie	S	D	N	A	N	A	6-9

Height up to 3 ft.

		BEST MONTH	POSITION	SOIL	LIGHT	MOISTURE LEVEL	DECIDUOUS/EVERGREEN	TYPE
Gaultheria shallon		S	E	W	S	A	E	5&10
Genista hispanica		S	E	D	F	N	E	5-6
Genista lydia		S	D	D	F	N	E	5-6
Hebe	Autumn Glory	S	E	D	FP	N	A	6-10
	Marjorie	S	E	N	FP	N	A	7-9
	Mrs. Winder	S	E	N	FP	N	A	11-3
Hebe albicans		S	E	N	FP	N	A	6-7
Hedera helix	Arborescens	S	E	A	A	N	A	1-12
Juniperus sabina	Blue Danube	C	E	A	A	N	E	1-12
	Rockery Gem	C	E	A	A	N	E	1-12
Juniperus scopulorum	Table Top Blue	C	E	A	A	N	E	1-12
Juniperus x media	Gold Coast	C	E	A	F	N	E	1-12
	Mint Julep	C	E	A	A	N	E	1-12
	Old Gold	C	E	A	FP	N	E	1-12
	Pfitzerana Aurea	C	E	A	FP	N	E	1-12
	Pfitzerana Glauca	C	E	A	A	N	E	1-12
	Pfitzerana	C	E	A	A	N	E	1-12
	Plumosa Aurea	C	E	A	FP	N	E	1-12
	Sulphur Spray	C	E	A	FP	N	E	1-12
Kalmia augustifolia	Rubra	S	E	W	P	A	A	6-7
Lavandula	Munstead	S	E	D	F	N	A	7-9
Ligustrum japonicum	Rotundifolium	S	E	N	A	N	A	1-12
Lonicera pileata		S	E	N	A	N	E	4-6
Mahonia aquifolium	Apollo	S	E	A	A	N	A	4-5

Height up to 3 ft.

		TYPE	DECIDUOUS/EVERGREEN	MOISTURE LEVEL	LIGHT	SOIL	POSITION	BEST MONTH
Philadelphus	Manteau d'Hermine	S	D	N	FP	N	A	6-7
Phormium tenax	Yellow Wave	S	D	A	F	N	A	1-12
Picea glauca	Albertiana Conica	C	E	N	A	N	A	1-12
Picea omorika	Nana	C	E	N	A	N	A	1-12
Picea pungens	Globosa	C	E	N	F	N	A	1-12
Pinus strobus	Nana	C	E	N	A	N	A	1-12
Pittosporum tenuifolium	Tom Thumb	S	E	N	FP	N	S	10-3
Potentilla x fruticosa	Daydawn	S	D	D	FP	N	E	5-9
	Longacre	S	D	D	FP	N	E	6-9
	Red Ace	S	D	D	FP	N	E	6-9
	Royal Flush	S	D	D	FP	N	E	6-9
	Sunset	S	D	D	FP	N	E	6-10
	Tangerine	S	D	D	FP	N	E	6-9
Prunus laurocerasus	Otto Luyken	S	E	D	A	N	S	11-4
Punica granatum	Nana	S	D	N	F	N	S	9-10
Rhododendron	Aksel Olsen	S	E	W	FP	A	A	5
	Antge	S	E	W	FP	A	A	5-6
	Baden Baden	S	E	W	FP	A	A	6
	Blitz	S	E	W	FP	A	A	5
	Blue Tit	S	E	W	FP	A	A	4-5
	Bremen	S	E	W	FP	A	A	5-6
	Carmen	S	E	W	FP	A	A	4
	Chikor	S	E	W	FP	A	A	4-5
	Humming Bird	S	E	W	FP	A	A	5

Height up to 3 ft.

		BEST MONTH	POSITION	SOIL	LIGHT	MOISTURE LEVEL	DECIDUOUS/EVERGREEN	TYPE
Rhododendron	Jewel	S	E	W	FP	A	A	6
	Linda	S	E	W	FP	A	A	5
	Scarlet Wonder	S	E	W	FP	A	A	5-6
Rhododendron fimbriatum		S	E	W	FP	A	A	4-5
Rhododendron praecox		S	E	W	FP	A	A	2-3
Rhododendron williamsianum		S	E	W	FP	A	A	4
Rhododendron x yakushimanum	Bambi	S	E	W	FP	A	A	5-6
Salvia officinalis	Purpurascens	S	E	D	F	N	S	5-9
Sarcococca confusa		S	E	N	A	C	A	2-3
Senecio	Sunshine (greyi)	S	E	D	F	N	A	5-10
Skimmia reevesiana		S	E	A	A	N	A	8-3
Spiraea japonica	Gold Flame	S	D	N	FP	N	A	4-6
	Golden Princess	S	D	N	FP	N	A	4-8
Spiraea nipponica tosaensis	(Snowmound)	S	D	N	FP	N	A	6
Spiraea x bumalda	Anthony Waterer	S	D	N	FP	N	A	6-9
Taxus baccata	Dovastonii Aurea	C	E	A	F	N	A	1-12
	Semperaurea	C	E	N	F	N	E	1-12
Thuja orientalis	Aurea Nana	C	E	N	F	N	A	1-12
Viburnum davidii		S	E	N	A	N	A	5&10
Viburnum opulus	Xanthocarpum	S	D	N	A	N	E	6&10
Vinca major		S	E	A	A	N	E	4-6
Vinca major	Variegata (Elegantissima)	S	E	A	A	N	E	4-6
Weigela florida	Foliis Purpureis	S	D	A	FP	N	A	5-6

Shrubs, Conifers and Heathers
to a Height of Four Foot

Height up to 4 ft.

		TYPE	DECIDUOUS/EVERGREEN	MOISTURE LEVEL	LIGHT	SOIL	POSITION	BEST MONTH
Abelia x grandiflora	Gold Sport	S	E	D	FP	N	S	6-9
Agave americana	Mediopicta	S	E	D	F	N	S	1-12
Azalea japonica	Gretchen	S	E	W	FP	A	A	5-6
	Orange Beauty	S	E	W	S	A	A	4-5
	Palestrina	S	E	W	S	A	A	4-5
Berberis candidula		S	E	N	FP	N	E	4-5
Berberis thunbergii	Aurea	S	D	N	P	N	A	4-6,
Berberis wilsoniae		S	D	N	FP	N	E	8-10
Caryopteris x clandonensis	Arthur Simmonds	S	D	D	F	N	A	6-9
Chamaecyparis lawsoniana	Ellwood's Gold	C	E	N	F	N	A	1-12
	Ellwoods Pillar	C	E	N	A	N	A	1-12
Chamaecyparis obtusa	Nana Aurea	C	E	N	F	N	A	4-11
Chamaecyparis pisifera	Boulevard	C	E	N	FP	N	A	1-12
	Plumosa Aurea Nana	C	E	N	F	N	A	1-12
	Squarrosa Lombarts	C	E	N	FP	N	A	1-12
Cistus	Sunset	S	E	D	F	N	A	6-7
Cistus purpureus		S	E	N	F	N	A	6-7
Cistus x corbariensis		S	E	D	F	N	A	5-6
Cytisus x praecox		S	D	D	F	N	A	4-5
Cytisus x praecox	Albus	S	D	D	F	N	A	4-5
Daphne mezereum		S	D	D	FP	C	A	2-3
Daphne x burkwoodii		S	E	N	FP	N	A	5-6
Erica erigena (mediterranea)	Irish Dusk	H	E	A	FP	N	E	12-3
Escallonia rubra	Woodside	S	E	A	FP	N	A	6-8

Height up to 4 ft.

		BEST MONTH	POSITION	SOIL	LIGHT	MOISTURE LEVEL	DECIDUOUS/EVERGREEN	TYPE
Fuchsia	Chillerton Beauty	S	D	A	A	N	A	6-9
	Drame	S	D	A	A	N	A	6-9
	Madame Cornelissen	S	D	N	A	N	A	6-9
	Margaret	S	D	N	A	N	A	6-9
	Mrs Popple	S	D	A	A	N	A	6-10
	Tennessee Waltz	S	D	N	A	N	A	7-10
Fuchsia magellanica		S	D	A	A	N	A	8-11
Fuchsia magellanica	Gracilis	S	D	N	A	A	A	8-11
	Versicolor (tricolor)	S	D	N	A	N	A	6-9
Genista tinctoria	Royal Gold	S	D	D	F	N	E	6-8
Hebe	Gauntletii	S	E	N	FP	N	S	7-8
	Great Orme	S	E	N	FP	N	A	7-8
	Purple Queen	S	E	N	FP	N	S	7-9
	Simon Delaux	S	E	N	FP	N	S	7-9
Hebe franciscana	Blue Gem	S	E	N	FP	N	A	6-10
Hebe veitchii		S	E	N	FP	N	S	7-9
Hydrangea serrata	Bluebird	S	D	W	S	A	A	7-9
Hypericum inodorum	Elstead	S	E	D	FP	N	A	7-9
Juniperus	Grey Owl	C	E	A	FP	N	E	1-12
Juniperus chinensis	Robusta Green	C	E	A	FP	N	A	1-12
Juniperus squamata	Meyeri	C	E	A	F	N	A	1-12
Lavandula	Vera	S	E	D	F	N	A	7-8
Mahonia aquifolium		S	E	A	A	N	E	3-4
Mahonia aquifolium	Moseri	S	E	A	A	N	E	3-4

Height up to 4 ft.

		BEST MONTH	POSITION	SOIL	LIGHT	MOISTURE LEVEL	DECIDUOUS/EVERGREEN	TYPE
Pernettya mucronata		S	E	W	A	A	A	8-11
Pernettya mucronata (Male)		S	E	W	A	A	A	5-6
Phygelius capensis		S	E	N	F	N	A	7-10
Phygelius capensis	Coccineus	S	E	N	F	N	S	7-10
	Winton Fanfare	S	E	N	F	N	S	7-10
Pieris japonica	Variegata	S	E	W	S	A	A	1-12
Pieris japonica (seedling)		S	E	W	S	A	A	1-12
Potentilla dahurica	Hersii	S	D	D	FP	N	E	6-10
Potentilla x fruticosa	Elizabeth	S	D	D	FP	N	E	6-10
	Goldfinger	S	D	D	FP	N	E	6-9
	Klondike	S	D	D	FP	N	E	6-10
	Primrose Beauty	S	D	D	FP	N	E	6-10
Prunus tenella		S	D	N	FP	N	A	4
Prunus tenella	Fire Hill	S	D	N	FP	N	A	4
Rhododendron	Gristede	S	E	W	FP	A	A	4-5
	Blue Diamond	S	E	W	FP	A	A	4
	Cary Ann	S	E	W	FP	A	A	5
	China Boy	S	E	W	FP	A	A	4-5
	Dora Amateis	S	E	W	FP	A	A	4
	Elizabeth	S	E	W	FP	A	A	4
	Osmar	S	E	W	FP	A	A	5
	Purple Pillow	S	E	W	FP	A	A	4-5
	Unique	S	E	W	FP	A	A	5-6
Rhododendron brachycarpum		S	E	W	FP	A	A	6-7

Height up to 4 ft.

		BEST MONTH	POSITION	SOIL	LIGHT	MOISTURE LEVEL	DECIDUOUS/EVERGREEN	TYPE
Rhododendron dichroanthum scyphocalyx		S	E	W	FP	A	A	5-6
Rhododendron eudoxum		S	E	W	FP	A	A	4-5
Rhododendron punctatum		S	E	N	FP	A	A	5
Rhododendron x yakushimanum	Bashful	S	E	W	FP	A	A	5-6
	Chelsea Seventy	S	E	W	FP	A	A	6-7
	Doc	S	E	W	FP	A	A	5-6
	Golden Torch	S	E	W	FP	A	A	5-6
	Hoppy	S	E	W	FP	A	A	5-6
	Pink Cherub	S	E	W	FP	A	A	5-6
	Sneezy	S	E	W	FP	A	A	5-6
	Titian Beauty	S	E	W	FP	A	A	5-6
	Vintage Rose	S	E	W	FP	A	A	5-6
Rhododendron yakushimanum		S	E	W	FP	A	A	5-6
Salix lanata		S	D	W	FP	N	A	3-4
Skimmia japonica	Foremanii	S	E	A	A	N	A	9-2
	Rubella	S	E	A	A	N	A	9-4
Syringa velutina (syn. palibiniana)		S	D	N	F	C	A	5-6
Thuja occidentalis	Sunkist	C	E	N	F	N	A	1-12
Ulex europaeus	Plenus	S	E	D	F	N	E	4-5
Viburnum opulus	Nanum	S	D	N	FP	N	A	9-10
Yucca filamentosa		S	E	D	F	N	A	7-8
Yucca gloriosa	Variegata	S	E	D	F	N	A	1-12

Shrubs, Conifers and Heathers
to a Height of Six Foot

Height up to 6 ft.

		BEST MONTH	POSITION	SOIL	LIGHT	MOISTURE LEVEL	DECIDUOUS/EVERGREEN	TYPE
Abelia	Edward Goucher	S	E	D	FP	N	S	7-9
Abelia x grandiflora		S	E	D	FP	N	S	7-9
Acer japonicum	Aconitifolium (Laciniatum)	S	D	W	FP	A	S	4-10
Acer palmatum	Dissectum Atropurpureum	S	D	W	FP	A	S	4-10
	Dissectum	S	D	W	FP	A	S	4-10
Acer palmatum dissectum	Crimson Queen	S	D	W	FP	A	S	4-10
Araucaria araucana		C	E	A	FP	N	A	1-12
Arundinaria viridistriata (auricoma)		S	E	W	A	N	A	1-12
Aucuba japonica	Crotonifolia (Crotonoides)	S	E	A	A	N	E	1-12
	Picturata	S	E	A	A	N	A	1-12
	Speckles	S	E	A	A	N	A	1-12
	Variegata	S	E	A	A	N	E	1-12
Azalea	Knap Hill Whitethroat	S	D	N	FP	A	A	5&10
Azalea mollis	Hortulanus H. Witte	S	D	W	FP	A	A	5&9
	Koningin Emma	S	D	W	FP	A	A	5&9
	Koster's Brilliant Red	S	D	W	FP	A	A	5&9
	Mathilda	S	D	W	FP	A	A	5&9
Azalea mollis Standard, Mixed colours		S	D	W	FP	A	A	5&9
Azalea mollis mixed colours		S	D	W	FP	A	A	5&9
Berberis thunbergii		S	D	N	A	N	E	4&9
Berberis thunbergii	Atropurpurea	S	D	N	A	N	E	4-10
	Harlequin	S	D	N	FP	N	E	4-10
	Helmond Pillar	S	D	N	FP	N	A	4-9

		TYPE	DECIDUOUS/EVERGREEN	MOISTURE LEVEL	LIGHT	SOIL	POSITION	BEST MONTH
Berberis thunbergii	Rose Glow	S	D	N	FP	N	E	4-10
Berberis verruculosa		S	E	N	FP	N	E	5-6
Berberis x lologensis	Apricot Queen	S	E	N	FP	N	E	4-5
Berberis x ottawensis	Gold Ring	S	D	N	FP	N	E	4-9
Buddleia davidii	Nanho Blue	S	D	D	F	N	A	7-9
Buxus sempervirens		S	E	N	A	N	E	1-12
Buxus sempervirens	Elegantissima	S	E	N	FP	N	E	1-12
Callistemon linearis		S	E	D	F	N	S	7-8
Camellia japonica	Alba Simplex	S	E	N	S	A	S	2-4
	Blood of China	S	E	N	S	A	S	2-4
	Bobs Tinsie	S	E	N	S	A	S	2-4
	Brushfields Yellow	S	E	N	S	A	S	2-4
	Dainty	S	E	N	S	A	S	3-4
	El Dorado	S	E	N	S	A	A	2-4
	Elegans	S	E	N	S	A	S	2-4
	Guest of Honour	S	E	N	S	A	A	2-4
	Guillio Nuccio	S	E	N	S	A	S	2-3
	Kick Off	S	E	N	S	A	S	2-4
	Kitty	S	E	N	S	A	A	2-4
	Mary Phoebe Taylor	S	E	N	S	A	S	2-3
	Shirobotan	S	E	N	S	A	S	2-4
	The Czar	S	E	N	S	A	S	2-4
Camellia sasanqua	Yuletide	S	E	N	S	A	S	11-12
Camellia x williamsii	Anticipation	S	E	N	S	A	A	2-4

Height up to 6 ft.

		BEST MONTH	POSITION	SOIL	LIGHT	MOISTURE LEVEL	DECIDUOUS/EVERGREEN	TYPE
Camellia x williamsii	Elegant Beauty	S	E	N	S	A	S	2-4
Caragana arborescens pendula	Walker	S	D	N	FP	N	E	5-6
Ceanothus thyrsiflorus repens		S	E	D	F	N	A	5-6
Ceanothus thyrsiflorus repens	Gnome	S	E	D	F	N	S	5-6
Chaenomeles x superba	Boule de Feu	S	D	A	A	N	E	2-4
	Etna	S	D	A	A	N	E	2-4
	Nicoline	S	D	A	A	N	E	2-4
Chamaecyparis lawsoniana	Blue Surprise	C	E	N	FP	N	A	1-12
	Chilworth Silver	C	E	N	FP	N	A	1-12
	Green Pillar	C	E	N	A	N	A	1-12
Chamaecyparis pisifera	Squarrosa Sulphurea	C	E	N	FP	N	A	4-9
Choisya ternata		S	E	A	FP	N	A	5-6
Cistus laurifolius		S	E	D	F	N	A	6-7
Corylopsis pauciflor		S	D	A	FP	A	A	3
Corylus avellana	Contorta	S	D	A	A	N	E	12-3
Cotinus coggygria	Notcutt's Variety	S	D	N	F	N	A	5-9
Cotoneaster dammeri	Coral Beauty (Short Stem)	S	E	A	FP	N	A	5&10
Cryptomeria japonica	Elegans	C	E	A	FP	N	A	1-12
Cytisus	Cornish Cream	S	D	D	F	N	E	5
	Daisy Hill	S	D	D	F	N	E	5-6
	Fulgens', Standard	S	D	D	F	N	A	6
	Golden Sunlight	S	D	D	F	N	E	5
	Goldfinch	S	D	D	F	N	E	5

Height up to 6 ft.

		BEST MONTH	POSITION	SOIL	LIGHT	MOISTURE LEVEL	DECIDUOUS/EVERGREEN	TYPE
Cytisus	Goldfinch, Standard	S	D	D	F	N	A	5
	Hollandia	S	D	D	F	N	E	4-5
	Killiney Red	S	D	D	F	N	E	5-6
	Queen Mary	S	D	D	F	N	E	5
	Redwings	S	D	D	F	N	A	5-6
	Zeelandia	S	D	D	F	N	E	5-6
	burkwoodii	S	D	D	F	N	A	5-6
Cytisus burkwoodii,	Standard	S	D	D	F	N	A	5-6
Cytisus scoparius	Andreanus	S	D	D	F	N	A	5-6
Cytisus x praecox,	Standard	S	D	D	F	N	A	4-5
Daphne odora	Aureomarginata	S	E	N	FP	N	S	2-4
	Walberton	S	E	N	FP	N	S	2-4
Deutzia	Mont Rose	S	D	A	FP	N	E	6
Deutzia gracilis	Rosea	S	D	A	FP	N	E	6
Deutzia x kalmiiflora		S	D	A	FP	N	E	6
Diervilla x splendens		S	D	A	FP	N	A	6-8
Erica lusitanica		H	E	A	F	A	S	1-4
Escallonia	Crimson Spire	S	E	A	FP	N	A	6-9
	Donard Radiance	S	E	A	FP	N	A	7-9
	Donard Star	S	E	A	P	N	S	6-7
	Red Elf	S	E	A	FP	N	A	6-9
Euonymus fortunei	Emerald 'n Gold (Short Stem)	S	E	A	A	N	A	1-12
	Emerald Gaiety (Short Stem)	S	E	A	A	N	A	1-12

24

Height up to 6 ft.

BEST MONTH POSITION SOIL LIGHT MOISTURE LEVEL DECIDUOUS/EVERGREEN TYPE								
Euonymus japonica	Ovatus Aureus	S	E	N	F	N	A	1-12
Fuchsia	Riccartonii	S	D	N	A	N	A	6-9
Fuchsia magellanica	Variegata	S	D	N	FP	N	6-9	
Hebe	Midsummer Beauty	S	E	N	F	N	S	7-9
Hebe salicifolia		S	E	N	FP	N	A	6-8
Hebe x andersonii	Variegata	S	E	N	F	N	S	8-9
Hydrangea	Blue Wave	S	D	W	A	N	A	6-8
Hydrangea hortensis	Alpengluchen	S	D	W	A	N	A	7-9
	Altona	S	D	W	A	N	A	6-8
	Blue Prince	S	D	W	A	N	A	7-9
	Chaperon Rouge	S	D	W	A	N	A	7-9
	Europa	S	D	W	A	N	A	7-9
	Gen. Vicomtesse de Vibraye	S	D	W	A	N	A	7-9
	Gertude Glahn	S	D	W	A	N	A	7-9
	Hamburg	S	D	W	A	N	A	7-9
	Heinrich Seidel	S	D	W	A	N	A	7-9
	King George	S	D	W	A	N	A	7-9
	Madame Emile Moulliere	S	D	W	A	N	A	7-9
Hydrangea hortensis (mixed)		S	D	W	A	N	A	7-9
Hydrangea serrata	Preziosa	S	D	W	A	N	A	7-10
Hypericum	Hidcote	S	E	A	FP	N	A	7-10
Hypericum beanii	Gold Cup	S	D	A	FP	N	S	6-9
Hypericum prolificum		S	E	A	FP	N	A	6-8
Ilex aquifolium	Argenteomarginata	S	E	N	A	N	A	1-12

25

Height up to 6 ft.

		BEST MONTH	POSITION	SOIL	LIGHT	MOISTURE LEVEL	DECIDUOUS/EVERGREEN	TYPE
Ilex aquifolium	Green Pillar	S	E	N	A	N	A	9-2
	J. C. van Tol	S	D	N	A	N	A	9-2
Ilex x altaclarensis	Golden King	S	E	N	A	N	A	1-12
Indigofera gerardiana		S	D	D	F	N	A	6-9
Itea virginica		S	D	W	A	N	S	7
Juniperus chinensis	Aurea	C	E	A	F	N	A	1-12
	Blue Point	C	E	A	FP	N	E	1-12
	Kuriwao Gold	C	E	A	FP	N	E	1-12
Juniperus communis	Wallis	C	E	A	A	N	E	1-12
Kalmia latifolia		S	E	W	FP	A	A	6
Kerria japonica	Variegata (Picta)	S	D	A	FP	N	A	4-5
Leycesteria formosa		S	D	D	A	N	A	6-9
Ligustrum ovalifolium	Argenteum	S	E	A	FP	N	A	1-12
	Aureum	S	E	A	FP	N	A	1-12
Lonicera nitida		S	E	D	FP	N	A	1-12
Lonicera nitida	Baggessen's Gold	S	E	D	FP	N	A	1-12
Magnolia	Suzan	S	D	W	FP	C	A	5-6
Magnolia stellata		S	D	W	FP	A	A	3-4
Magnolia stellata	Rosea	S	D	W	FP	A	A	3-4
Myrtus apiculata	Glen Gleam	S	E	N	FP	N	S	8-9
Myrtus communis	Tarentina	S	E	N	FP	N	S	7-8
Nandina domestica		S	E	A	F	N	S	9-10
Olearia haastii		S	E	D	FP	N	A	7-8
Osmanthus delavayi		S	E	N	FP	N	A	4

Height up to 6 ft.

		BEST MONTH	POSITION	SOIL	LIGHT	MOISTURE LEVEL	DECIDUOUS/EVERGREEN	TYPE
Osmanthus heterophyllus	Variegatus	S	E	N	FP	N	A	1-12
Osmarea Burkwoodii		S	E	N	FP	N	A	4-5
Paeonia suffruticosa (arborea)		S	D	W	FP	N	A	5
Perovskia atriplicifolia	Blue Spire	S	D	N	F	N	A	6-9
Philadelphus	Belle Etoile	S	D	A	FP	N	A	6-7
Philadelphus coronarius	Aureus	S	D	A	FP	N	A	6-7
Phlomis fruticosa		S	D	D	F	N	S	6-7
Phormium tenax	Purpureum	S	E	A	FP	N	S	1-12
	Variegatum	S	E	A	F	N	A	1-12
Picea brewerana		C	E	N	A	N	A	1-12
Picea pungens	Moerheimii	C	E	N	F	N	A	1-12
Pieris Forest	Flame	S	E	W	S	A	A	1-12
Pieris japonica	Purity	S	E	W	S	A	A	1-12
Pieris taiwanensis		S	E	W	S	A	A	1-12
Pinus aristata		C	E	N	FP	N	A	1-12
Pinus mugo		C	E	N	A	N	E	1-12
Pinus sylvestris	Aurea	C	E	N	F	N	A	10-3
	Nana	C	E	A	A	N	E	1-12
	Watereri	C	E	N	FP	N	E	1-12
Potentilla x fruticosa	Golddigger	S	D	D	FP	N	E	6-9
	Katherine Dykes	S	D	D	FP	N	E	6-10
Prunus	Cistena	S	D	N	FP	N	A	4-10
Prunus laurocerasus	Castlewellan	S	E	A	FP	N	A	4
Pyracantha coccinea	Harlequin	S	E	A	FP	N	E	5&10

Height up to 6 ft.

		BEST MONTH	POSITION	SOIL	LIGHT	MOISTURE LEVEL	DECIDUOUS/EVERGREEN	TYPE
Rhododendron	America	S	E	W	FP	A	A	5-6
	Britannia	S	E	W	FP	A	A	5-6
	Chevalier Felix de Sauvage	S	E	W	FP	A	A	5-6
	Cosmopolitan	S	E	W	FP	A	A	5-6
	Cunningham's White	S	E	W	FP	A	A	5-6
	Doncaster	S	E	W	FP	A	A	5
	Dr. A.W. Endtz	S	E	W	FP	A	A	5-6
	Dr. H.C. Dresselhuys	S	E	W	FP	A	A	5-6
	Dr. V.H. Rutgers	S	E	W	FP	A	A	5-6
	Edward Rand	S	E	W	FP	A	A	5-6
	Elsie Straver	S	E	W	FP	A	A	5-6
	Fabia	S	E	W	FP	A	A	5-6
	Fastuosum Flore Pleno	S	E	W	FP	A	A	5-6
	Goldsworth Orange	S	E	W	FP	A	S	6
	Hugo Koster	S	E	W	FP	A	A	5-6
	Kate Waterer	S	E	W	FP	A	A	5-6
	Lady Clementine Mitford	S	E	W	FP	A	A	6
	Lavender Girl	S	E	W	FP	A	A	5
	Lord Roberts	S	E	W	FP	A	A	5
	Moerheim Pink	S	E	W	FP	A	A	4-5
	Mrs T.H. Lowinsky	S	E	W	FP	A	A	6
	Nova Zembla	S	E	W	FP	A	A	5-6
	Pink Pearl	S	E	W	FP	A	A	5-6
	Prince Camille de Rohan	S	E	W	FP	A	A	5-6

Height up to 6 ft.

		BEST MONTH	POSITION	SOIL	LIGHT	MOISTURE LEVEL	DECIDUOUS/EVERGREEN	TYPE
Rhododendron	Rose Ann Whitney	S	E	W	FP	A	A	5-6
	Sappho	S	E	W	FP	A	A	5-6
	Van Weerden Poelman	S	E	W	FP	A	A	5-6
	Wilgens Ruby	S	E	W	FP	A	A	5-6
	Winsome	S	E	W	FP	A	A	5
Rhododendron ponticum	Variegatum	S	E	W	FP	A	A	1-12
Romneya x hybrida		S	D	D	FP	N	A	7-9
Rosmarinus officinalis		S	E	D	F	N	A	5
Salix hastata	Wehrhahnii	S	D	W	A	N	E	2-4
Sambucus racemosa	Plumosa Aurea	S	D	A	FP	N	A	5-8
Spiraea cinerea	Grefsheim	S	D	N	FP	N	E	4-5
Spiraea thunbergii		S	D	N	FP	N	E	3-4
Spiraea x vanhouttei		S	D	N	FP	N	E	6
Symphoricarpos albus		S	D	A	A	N	E	9-2
Symphoricarpos orbiculatus	Variegatus	S	D	A	F	N	A	5-11
Syringa microphylla	Superba	S	D	N	FP	C	A	5
Taxus baccata		C	E	N	A	N	E	1-12
Taxus baccata	Standishii	C	E	N	F	N	A	1-12
Teucrium fruticans		S	E	N	F	N	S	6-9
Thuja occidentalis	Holmstrupii	C	E	N	A	N	A	1-12
	Lutea Nana	C	E	N	F	N	A	1-12
	Rheingold	C	E	N	F	N	A	1-12
Thuja orientalis	Elegantissma	C	E	N	F	N	A	1-12
Vaccinium corymbosum		S	D	W	FP	A	S	7-10

Height up to 6 ft.

		BEST MONTH	POSITION	SOIL	LIGHT	MOISTURE LEVEL	DECIDUOUS/EVERGREEN	TYPE
Vaccinium corymbosum	Blue Ray	S	D	W	FP	A	A	7-8
	Grover	S	D	W	FP	A	A	9
Vestia foetida		S	E	N	F	N	S	4-7
Viburnum carlesii	Aurora	S	D	N	FP	N	A	4-5
Viburnum plicatum	Watanabei	S	D	N	FP	N	A	7-8
Viburnum tinus	Eve Price	S	E	N	A	N	A	9-3
	Gwenllian	S	E	N	A	N	A	9-3
Viburnum x carlcephalum		S	D	N	FP	N	A	5
Viburnum x juddii		S	D	N	FP	N	A	4-5
Weigela florida	Variegata	S	D	A	FP	N	A	5-6

Shrubs, Conifers and Heathers
to a Height above Six Foot

		TYPE	DECIDUOUS/EVERGREEN	MOISTURE LEVEL	LIGHT	SOIL	POSITION	BEST MONTH
Abies koreana		C	E	A	FP	N	A	1-12
Abutilon vitifolium		S	D	D	F	N	S	5-7
Acer griseum		S	D	N	FP	N	A	1-12
Acer negundo	Flamingo	S	D	W	FP	N	S	4-9
Acer palmatum		S	D	W	FP	A	A	4-10
Acer palmatum	Aureum	S	D	W	FP	A	S	4-9
	Bloodgood	S	D	W	FP	A	A	5-9
	Heptalobum Osakazuki	S	D	W	FP	A	A	9-10
	Senkaki	S	D	W	FP	N	A	1-12
	Atropurpureum	S	D	W	FP	A	A	4-9
Amelanchier canadensis	(Lamarckii)	S	D	W	FP	A	A	5&10
Aralia elata	Aureovariegata	S	D	D	FP	N	A	4-9
	Variegata	S	D	D	FP	N	A	4-9
Arbutus unedo		S	E	A	FP	N	A	8-10
Aronia arbutifolia		S	D	W	FP	A	A	4&9
Arundinaria japonica		S	E	W	A	N	A	5-9
Arundinaria murieliae		S	E	W	A	N	A	1-12
Arundinaria nitida		S	E	W	A	N	A	1-12
Azalea	Knap Hill Brazil	S	D	W	FP	A	A	5
	Gibraltar	S	D	W	FP	A	A	5
	Glowing Embers	S	D	W	FP	A	A	5&10
	Gog	S	D	W	FP	A	A	5
	Homebush	S	D	W	FP	A	A	5-6
	Kathleen	S	D	W	FP	A	A	5

Height above 6 ft.

		TYPE	DECIDUOUS/EVERGREEN	MOISTURE LEVEL	LIGHT	SOIL	POSITION	BEST MONTH
Azalea	Satan	S	D	W	FP	A	A	5-6
	Silver Slipper	S	D	W	FP	A	A	5-6
Berberis darwinii		S	E	N	FP	N	E	4-5
Berberis julianae		S	E	N	FP	N	E	5-6
Berberis linearifolia	Orange King	S	E	N	FP	N	A	4-5
Berberis x ottawensis	Purpurea	S	D	N	FP	N	E	4-9
Berberis x stenophylla		S	E	D	FP	N	E	4-5
Buddleia	Lochinch	S	D	D	F	N	A	7-9
Buddleia alternifolia		S	D	D	F	N	A	6
Buddleia davidii	Black Knight	S	D	D	F	N	A	7-9
	Border Beauty	S	D	D	F	N	A	7-9
	Empire Blue	S	D	D	F	N	A	7-9
	Fascination	S	D	D	F	N	A	7-9
	Harlequin	S	D	D	F	N	A	7-9
	Ile de France	S	D	D	F	N	A	7-9
	Royal Red	S	D	D	F	N	A	7-9
	White Bouquet	S	D	D	F	N	A	7-9
	White Cloud	S	D	D	F	N	A	7-9
	White Profusion	S	D	D	F	N	A	7-9
Buddleia globosa		S	E	D	F	N	A	5-6
Callicarpa bodinieri	Profusion	S	D	N	FP	N	A	8-12
Camellia japonica	Billie McFarland	S	E	N	S	A	S	2-4
	Brigadoon	S	E	N	S	A	S	2-4

Height above 6 ft.

		TYPE	DECIDUOUS/EVERGREEN	MOISTURE LEVEL	LIGHT	SOIL	POSITION	BEST MONTH
Camellia japonica	Diamond Head	S	E	N	S	A	S	2-4
	Flame	S	E	N	S	A	S	2-4
	Grand Prix	S	E	N	S	A	S	2-4
	Jury's Yellow	S	E	N	S	A	S	2-4
	Lady Clare	S	E	N	S	A	S	2-4
	Laura Walker	S	E	N	S	A	S	2-4
	Margaret Davies	S	E	N	S	A	S	2-4
	Powder Puff	S	E	A	S	A	S	2-4
	Red Ensign	S	E	N	S	A	S	2-4
Camellia x williamsii	Ballet Queen	S	E	N	S	A	S	2-4
	Barbara Clark	S	E	N	S	A	S	2-4
	Daintiness	S	E	N	S	A	S	2-4
	Debbie	S	E	N	S	A	S	3-4
	Donation	S	E	N	S	A	S	12-2
	Shocking pink	S	E	N	S	A	S	2-4
	Waterlily	S	E	N	S	A	S	2-4
Caragana arborescens		S	D	N	F	N	E	5
Catalpa bignonioides	Aurea	S	D	N	FP	N	S	5-8
Ceanothus	A.T. Johnson	S	E	N	F	N	S	5&9
	Autumnal Blue	S	E	N	F	N	A	7-9
	Burkwoodii	S	E	N	F	N	S	7-9
	Cascade	S	E	N	F	N	S	5
	Delight	S	E	N	F	N	A	5
	Gloire de Versailles	S	D	N	F	N	A	7-10

Height above 6 ft.

	BEST MONTH POSITION SOIL LIGHT MOISTURE LEVEL DECIDUOUS/EVERGREEN TYPE							
Ceanothus	Puget Blue	S	E	N	F	N	S	5-6
Ceanothus dentatus		S	E	N	F	N	S	5
Ceanothus impressus		S	E	N	F	N	S	5-6
Ceanothus x veitchianus		S	E	N	F	N	S	5-6
Cedrus atlantica	Glauca	C	E	N	FP	N	A	1-12
Cedrus deodara		C	E	N	FP	N	A	1-12
Cedrus deodara	Aurea	C	E	N	F	N	A	4-8
Cedrus libani		C	E	N	FP	N	A	1-12
Cephalanthus occidentalis		S	D	A	FP	N	E	8
Cercidiphyllum japonicum		S	D	N	FP	N	A	8-10
Cercis	Forest Pansy	S	D	N	F	N	A	5-9
Cercis siliquastrum		S	D	N	F	N	A	5&9
Chaenomeles speciosa	Nivalis	S	D	A	A	N	E	2-4
	Rubra	S	D	A	A	N	E	2-4
	Sargentii	S	D	A	A	N	E	2-4
Chaenomeles x superba	Crimson and Gold	S	D	A	A	N	E	2-4
	Elly Mossel	S	D	A	A	N	E	2-4
	Fire Dance	S	D	A	A	N	E	2-4
	Knap Hill Scarlet	S	D	A	A	N	E	2-4
	Pink Lady	S	D	A	A	N	E	2-4
	Rowallane	S	D	A	A	N	E	2-4
	Vermilion	S	D	A	A	N	E	2-4
Chamaecyparis lawsoniana		C	E	N	A	N	A	1-12
Chamaecyparis lawsoniana	Allumii Gold	C	E	N	F	N	A	1-12

Height above 6 ft.

		BEST MONTH	POSITION	SOIL	LIGHT	MOISTURE LEVEL	DECIDUOUS/EVERGREEN	TYPE	
Chamaecyparis lawsoniana	Allumii	C	E	N	A	N	A		4-9
	Broomhill Gold	C	E	N	F	N	A		1-12
	Columnaris Glauca	C	E	N	FP	N	A		1-12
	Ellwoodii	C	E	N	A	N	A		1-12
	Erecta	C	E	W	A	N	A		1-12
	Fletcheri	C	E	N	A	N	A		1-12
	Golden Wonder	C	E	N	F	N	A		1-12
	Green Hedger	C	E	N	A	N	A		1-12
	Lane	C	E	N	F	N	A		1-12
	New Golden Seedling	C	E	W	F	N	A		1-12
	Pembury Blue	C	E	N	FP	N	A		1-12
	Pottenii	C	E	N	A	N	A		1-12
	Stardust	C	E	N	F	N	A		1-12
	Stewartii	C	E	N	F	N	A		1-12
	Yellow Transparent	C	E	N	F	N	A		1-12
Chimonanthus praecox		S	D	N	FP	N	S		12-2
Colutea arborescens	Copper Beauty	S	D	D	F	N	E		6-10
Cordyline australis		S	E	D	F	N	S		1-12
Cornus alba	Elegantissima	S	D	W	A	N	E		1-12
	Sibirica (Westonbirt)	S	D	W	A	N	E		11-3
	Spaethii (Gouchaltii)	S	D	W	A	N	E		1-12
Cornus controversa		S	D	W	FP	N	E		5&10
Cornus florida		S	D	W	FP	N	A		5&10
Cornus florida	Rainbow	S	D	W	FP	N	A		5-10

Height above 6 ft.

		BEST MONTH	POSITION	SOIL	LIGHT	MOISTURE LEVEL	DECIDUOUS/EVERGREEN	TYPE
Cornus kousa		S	D	W	FP	N	A	6&10
Cornus kousa chinensis		S	D	W	FP	N	A	6
Cornus mas		S	D	W	FP	N		2&9
Cornus nuttallii		S	D	W	FP	N	A	5&9
Cornus stonolifera	Flaviramea	S	D	W	A	N	E	10-3
Coronilla emerus		S	D	D	FP	N	A	6-9
Cortaderia argentea (selloana)		S	D	A	FP	N	A	8-10
Cortaderia selloana	Gold Band	S	D	A	FP	N	A	8-10
	Rosea	S	D	A	FP	N	A	8-10
Corylopsis willmottiae	Spring Purple	S	D	A	FP	A	A	3-8
Corylus avellana		S	D	N	FP	N	E	2-3
Corylus maxima	Purpurea	S	D	N	F	N	A	4-8
Cotinus coggygria		S	D	N	FP	N	A	6-10
Cotinus coggygria	Royal Purple	S	D	N	FP	N	A	4-10
Cotoneaster	Cornubia	S	E	A	FP	N	A	6&10
	John Waterer	S	E	A	FP	N	E	6&10
	Rothschildianus	S	E	A	FP	N	E	6&10
Cotoneaster franchetii		S	E	A	A	N	E	6-12
Cotoneaster horizontalis		S	D	A	A	N	E	8-2
Cotoneaster horizontalis	Variegatus	S	D	A	A	N	E	5-2
Cotoneaster lacteus		S	E	A	A	N	A	9-1
Cotoneaster salicifolius		S	E	A	A	N	A	6&10
Cotoneaster x watereri		S	E	A	FP	N	E	6&10
Crataegus monogyna		S	D	D	A	N	A	5&10

Height above 6 ft.

		BEST MONTH	POSITION	SOIL	LIGHT	MOISTURE LEVEL	DECIDUOUS/EVERGREEN	TYPE
Crinodendron hookeranum		S	E	N	P	A	S	5
Cupressocyparis leylandii		C	E	A	F	N	E	1-12
Cupressocyparis leylandii	Castlewellan	C	E	A	FP	N	E	1-12
Cupressus macrocarpa	Donard Gold	C	E	N	F	N	A	1-12
	Goldcrest	C	E	N	F	N	A	1-12
Cytisus	Dragonfly	S	D	D	F	N	A	5-6
	Minstead	S	D	D	F	N	E	5-6
	Windlesham Ruby	S	D	D	F	N	E	5-6
Cytisus battandieri		S	E	N	F	N	S	7
Deutzia magnifica		S	D	A	FP	N	A	6
Deutzia scabra	Plena	S	D	A	FP	N	E	6
Elaeagnus ebbingei		S	E	A	A	N	E	8-9
Elaeagnus pungens	Maculata	S	E	A	FP	N	E	1-12
Elaeagnus x ebbingei	Limelight	S	D	A	FP	N	A	8-9
Embothrium coccineum	Longifolium	S	E	N	F	A	S	5-6
Enkianthus campanulatus		S	D	W	FP	A	A	5&9
Erica arborea		H	E	A	F	A	S	4
Escallonia	Apple Blossom	S	E	A	FP	N	S	7-9
	C.F.Ball	S	E	A	FP	N	S	8-9
	Donard Seedling	S	E	A	FP	N	S	6-9
	Iveyi	S	E	A	FP	N	S	8-10
	Langleyensis	S	E	A	FP	N	S	6-9
	Pride of Donard	S	E	A	FP	N	S	8-9
Escallonia macrantha		S	E	A	FP	N	S	6-9

Height above 6 ft.

Name	Cultivar	TYPE	DECIDUOUS/EVERGREEN	MOISTURE LEVEL	LIGHT	SOIL	POSITION	BEST MONTH
Eucalyptus gunnii		S	E	N	FP	N	A	1-12
Eucryphia x nymansensis	Nymansay	S	E	N	P	A	S	8-9
Euonymus alatus (alata)		S	D	A	FP	N	E	9-11
Euonymus europaeus	Red Cascade	S	D	A	A	N	A	9-11
Euonymus fortunei	Silver Queen	S	E	A	FP	N	A	1-12
Euonymus japonica	Albomarginatus	S	E	D	A	N	S	1-12
Euonymus japonicus	Aureopictus	S	E	D	A	N	A	1-12
Fagus sylvatica		S	D	N	A	N	E	5&10
Fagus sylvatica	Purpurea	S	D	D	FP	N	E	5&10
Fatsia japonica	Variegata	S	E	N	P	N	S	4-10
Fatsia japonica (Aralia sieboldii)		S	E	N	A	N	S	5-10
Forsythia	Lynwood	S	D	A	FP	N	E	3
Forsythia x intermedia	Spectabilis	S	D	A	FP	N	E	3
Fothergilla major		S	D	W	FP	A	A	4&10
Fremontodendron	California Glory	S	E	D	F	C	S	6-9
Garrya elliptica		S	E	A	A	N	A	1-2
Garrya elliptica	James Roof	S	E	A	A	N	A	1-2
Genista aetnesis		S	D	D	F	N	A	6
Ginkgo biloba		C	D	N	FP	N	A	9-10
Griselinia littoralis		S	E	N	FP	N	S	5-8
Griselinia littoralis	Variegata	S	E	N	FP	N	S	5-8
Hamamelis mollis		S	D	N	FP	N	A	12-3
Hamamelis mollis	Pallida	S	D	N	FP	N	A	12-2

Height above 6 ft.

		BEST MONTH	POSITION	SOIL	LIGHT	MOISTURE LEVEL	DECIDUOUS/EVERGREEN	TYPE
Hamamelis x intermedia	Diane	S	D	N	FP	N	A	10-3
Hibiscus syriacus	Blue Bird	S	D	N	F	N	A	7-10
	Coelestis	S	D	N	F	N	A	7-10
	Hamabo	S	D	N	F	N	A	7-10
	Monstrosus	S	D	N	F	N	A	7-10
	Red Heart	S	D	N	F	N	A	8-9
	Woodbridge	S	D	N	F	N	A	7-10
Hydrangea aspera		S	D	W	P	N	S	6-7
Hydrangea paniculata	Grandiflora	S	D	N	FP	N	A	8-9
Hydrangea villosa		S	D	W	P	N	S	7-9
Ilex aquifolium		S	E	D	A	N	A	1-12
Ilex aquifolium	Handsworth New Silver	S	E	D	A	N	A	9-2
	Pyramidalis	S	E	D	A	N	A	9-2
	Silver Milkboy	S	E	D	A	N	A	1-12
	Silver Queen	S	E	N	A	N	A	1-12
Ilex myrtifolia		S	E	D	A	N	A	1-12
Ilex verticillata		S	D	D	A	N	A	10-1
Ilex x altaclarensis	Camelliifolia	S	E	D	A	N	A	9-2
Jasminum nudiflorum		S	D	N	A	N	A	11-2
Juniperus chinensis	Pyramidalis (Stricta)	C	E	N	F	N	A	1-12
Juniperus communis	Hibernica	C	E	N	FP	N	E	1-12
Juniperus scopulorum	Blue Heaven	C	E	N	FP	N	A	1-12
	Blue Pyramidal	C	E	N	FP	N	A	1-12
	Skyrocket	C	E	N	FP	N	A	1-12

Height above 6 ft.

	BEST MONTH	POSITION	SOIL	LIGHT	MOISTURE LEVEL	DECIDUOUS/EVERGREEN	TYPE
Juniperus virginiana	Burkii	C	E	N	FP	N	E	1-12
	Helle	C	E	N	FP	N	E	1-12
Kerria japonica		S	D	A	A	N	E	4-5
Kerria japonica	Pleniflora	S	D	A	A	N	E	4-5
Kolkwitzia amabilis		S	D	D	FP	N	E	5-6
Laburnum alpinum	Pendulum	S	D	D	FP	N	A	6
Laburnum x watereri	Vossii	S	D	D	FP	N	A	5
Larix decidua		C	D	N	A	N	E	4-9
Larix kaempferi	Pendula	C	D	N	FP	N	A	4-10
Lavatera olbia		S	D	D	F	N	A	6-10
Leucothoe fontanesiana	Rainbow	S	E	W	S	A	A	1-12
Ligustrum ovalifolium		S	E	A	A	N	A	7
Lonicera fragrantissima		S	E	A	FP	N	A	12-3
Magnolia grandiflora		S	E	N	FP	A	A	7-9
Magnolia grandiflora	Exmouth	S	E	N	FP	A	A	7-9
Magnolia liliiflora	Nigra	S	D	N	FP	A	A	4-6
Magnolia sieboldii		S	D	N	FP	A	S	5-6
Magnolia x proctoriana		S	D	N	FP	A	A	4
Magnolia x soulangiana		S	D	N	FP	A	A	4-5
Magnolia x soulangiana	Rustica Rubra	S	D	N	FP	A	A	4-5
Mahonia	Charity	S	E	A	FP	N	A	9-11
Mahonia bealei		S	E	A	FP	N	A	1-12
Mahonia japonica		S	E	A	FP	N	A	1-12
Malus	John Downie	S	D	N	FP	N	A	4&9

Height above 6 ft.

		TYPE	DECIDUOUS/EVERGREEN	MOISTURE LEVEL	LIGHT	SOIL	POSITION	BEST MONTH
Malus floribunda		S	D	N	FP	N	A	4
Metasequoia glyptostroboides		C	D	W	FP	N	A	4-9
Myrtus communis		S	E	N	FP	N	S	7-8
Olearia macrodonta		S	E	D	FP	N	A	7-8
Parrotia persica		S	D	N	FP	A	A	9-10
Philadelphus	Beauclerk	S	D	N	FP	N	A	6-7
	Virginal	S	D	N	FP	N	A	6-7
Philadelphus coronarius	Variegatus	S	D	N	FP	N	A	6-7
Phormium tenax		S	E	A	FP	N	S	1-12
Photinia glabra	Rubens	S	E	N	FP	N	A	4-9
Photinia x frazeri	Red Robin	S	E	N	FP	N	A	1-12
Picea abies		C	E	N	A	N	E	1-12
Picea abies	Frohburg	C	E	N	A	N	A	1-12
Picea omorika		C	E	N	A	N	E	1-12
Picea orientalis	Aurea (Aureospicata)	C	E	N	F	N	A	1-12
Picea pungens	Hoopsii	C	E	N	F	N	A	1-12
	Koster	C	E	N	F	N	A	1-12
Pieris formosa forestii		S	E	W	S	A	S	4-7
Pieris formosa forrestii	Wakehurst	S	E	W	S	A	A	1-12
Pieris japonica		S	E	W	S	A	A	1-12
Pinus nigra		C	E	N	A	N	E	1-12
Pinus parviflora	Glauca	C	E	N	FP	N	A	1-12
	Tempelhof	C	E	N	FP	N	A	1-12
Pinus sylvestris		C	E	N	FP	N	E	1-12

Height above 6 ft.

Name	Variety	TYPE	DECIDUOUS/EVERGREEN	MOISTURE LEVEL	LIGHT	SOIL	POSITION	BEST MONTH
Pinus wallichiana (Griffithii)		C	E	N	FP	N	A	1-12
Pittosporum tenuifolium		S	E	N	FP	N	A	1-12
Pittosporum tenuifolium	Arundel Green	S	E	N	FP	N	A	1-12
	Garnettii	S	E	N	FP	N	A	1-12
	Purpureum	S	E	N	FP	N	S	10-3
	Silver Queen	S	E	N	FP	N	A	1-12
Prunus Kanzan		S	D	N	FP	N	A	4
Prunus cerasifera	Nigra	S	D	N	FP	N	A	3-9
	Pissardii	S	D	N	FP	N	A	3-9
Prunus laurocerasus	Rotundifolia	S	E	N	A	N	A	4
Prunus lusitanica		S	E	N	A	N	E	6
Prunus lusitanica	Variegata	S	E	N	A	N		1-12
Prunus serrulata	Amanogawa	S	D	N	FP	N	A	4-5
Prunus subhirtella	Autumnalis Rosea	S	D	N	FP	N	A	11-3
Prunus triloba		S	D	N	FP	N	A	3-4
Pyracantha	Golden Charmer	S	E	A	A	N	E	5&10
	Mohave	S	E	A	A	N	E	5&10
	Orange Charmer	S	E	A	A	N	E	5&10
	Orange Glow	S	E	A	A	N	E	5&10
	Teton	S	E	A	A	N	E	5&10
	Yellow Charmer	S	E	A	A	N	E	5&10
	Yellow Sun	S	E	A	A	N	A	5&10
Rhododendron	Albert Schweitzer	S	E	W	FP	A	A	4-5
	Caractacus	S	E	W	FP	A	A	5

Height above 6 ft.

		TYPE	DECIDUOUS/EVERGREEN	MOISTURE LEVEL	LIGHT	SOIL	POSITION	BEST MONTH
Rhododendron	Cynthia	S	E	W	FP	A	A	5-6
	Dr. Tjebbes	S	E	W	FP	A	A	5-6
	Everastianum	S	E	W	FP	A	A	6
	Gomer Waterer	S	E	W	FP	A	A	6
	Harvest Moon	S	E	W	FP	A	A	5
	John Walter	S	E	W	FP	A	A	5-6
	Madame Masson	S	E	W	FP	A	A	5
	Peter Koster	S	E	W	FP	A	A	6
	Purple Splendour	S	E	W	FP	A	A	5
	Roseum Elegans	S	E	W	FP	A	E	5-6
Rhododendron catawbiense		S	E	W	FP	A	A	6
Rhododendron luteum (Azalea pontica)		S	D	W	FP	A	A	5&10
Rhododendron ponticum		S	E	W	FP	A	E	5-6
Rhus typhina		S	D	A	FP	N	A	9-10
Rhus typhina	Laciniata	S	D	A	FP	N	E	9-10
Ribes sanguineum	King Edward VII	S	D	A	FP	N	E	4
	Pulborough Scarlet	S	D	A	FP	N	E	3-4
Robinia hispida	Rosea	S	D	D	F	N	S	5-6
Romneya coulteri		S	D	N	F	N	S	7-10
Salix sachalinensis	Sekka	S	D	W	A	N	E	10-4
Sophora japonica		S	D	D	F	N	A	8-10
Sorbaria aitchisonii		S	D	N	FP	N	A	7-8
Sorbus	Kirsten Pink	S	D	N	FP	N	A	5-10

Height above 6 ft.

		TYPE	DECIDUOUS/EVERGREEN	MOISTURE LEVEL	LIGHT	SOIL	POSITION	BEST MONTH
Spartium junceum		S	D	D	F	N	A	7-9
Spiraea nipponica		S	D	N	FP	N	E	6
Spiraea x arguta		S	D	N	FP	N	E	4-5
Stranvaesia davidiana		S	E	N	A	N	A	6&10
Stranvinia	Redstart	S	E	A	FP	N	A	4&10
Symphoricarpos x doorenbosii		S	D	A	A	N	E	9-2
Symphoricarpos x doorenbosii	White Hedge	S	D	A	A	N	E	9-2
Syringa microphylla	Superba (Standard)	S	D	A	FP	N	A	5
Syringa reflexa		S	D	A	FP	N	A	5-6
Syringa vulgaris	Charles Joly	S	D	A	FP	N	A	5-6
	Katherine Havermeyer	S	D	A	FP	N	A	5-6
	Madame Lemoine	S	D	A	FP	N	A	5-6
	Primrose	S	D	A	FP	N	A	5-6
Syringa x prestoniae	Elinor	S	D	A	FP	N	A	5-6
Tamarix pentandra		S	D	D	FP	N	E	7-9
Tamarix tetrandra		S	D	D	FP	N	E	5-6
Taxus baccata	Fastigiata Aurea	C	E	N	F	N	A	1-12
	Fastigiata	C	E	N	A	N	A	1-12
Thuja occidentalis	Europe Gold	C	E	N	F	N	E	1-12
	Holmstrup Yellow	C	E	N	F	N	A	1-12
	Smaragd	C	E	N	A	N	A	1-12
Thuja orientalis	Conspicua	C	E	N	F	N	A	1-12

Height above 6 ft.

		BEST MONTH	POSITION	SOIL	LIGHT	MOISTURE LEVEL	DECIDUOUS/EVERGREEN	TYPE
Thuja plicata	Atrovirens	C	E	N	A	N	A	1-12
	Atrovirens	C	E	W	A	N	A	1-12
	Fastigiata	C	E	N	A	N	A	1-12
	Zebrina	C	E	N	FP	N	A	1-12
Thujopsis dolobrata		C	E	N	A	N	E	1-12
Tsuga heterophylla		C	E	N	A	N	A	1-12
Viburnum opulus		S	D	N	A	N	E	5&9
Viburnum opulus	Fructuluteo	S	D	N	A	N	E	6&9
	Sterile	S	D	N	FP	N	E	5-6
Viburnum plicatum	Lanarth	S	D	N	FP	N	A	5-6
	Mariesii	S	D	N	FP	N	A	5-6
	Pink Beauty	S	D	N	FP	N	A	5-6
Viburnum plicatum tomentosum		S	D	N	FP	N	A	5-6
Viburnum rhytidophyllum		S	E	N	FP	N	A	5
Viburnum tinus		S	E	N	A	N	A	9-3
Viburnum x bodnantense	Dawn	S	D	N	FP	N	A	10-2
Viburnum x burkwoodii		S	E	N	FP	N	A	4-5
Weigela	Abel Carriere	S	D	A	FP	N	A	5-6
	Bristol Ruby	S	D	A	FP	N	A	5-6
	Newport Red (Vanicek)	S	D	A	FP	N	A	5-6

PLANT DESCRIPTIONS
SHRUBS, CONIFERS, HEATHERS

Abelia 'Edward Goucher'

A hybrid raised at Glenn Dale, U.S.A. between A.x grandiflora and A. schumannii. An outstanding summer to autumn flowering shrub with deep lilac pink flowers. The foliage is brilliant dark green like its grandiflora parent. It would make an interesting tub specimen and is a first class plant for the smaller garden providing it is sheltered from cold winds.

Abelia x grandiflora

A small semi evergreen shrub suitable for the smaller garden. A hybrid between A. chinensis and A. uniflora which has acquired a vigour and constitution superior to either parent. The flowers are white tinged pink and funnel shaped. The foliage is brilliant dark green. A very desirable plant, provided it is given some protection from cold winds. Award of merit 1962.

Abelia x grandiflora 'Gold Sport'

A small semi evergreen flowering shrub. A selected form with a deep gold margin to the green leaves. The pale pink flowers are produced over a long period from summer through to autumn. An excellent shrub for the small garden, providing it is not exposed to cold winds.

Abies balsamea

A very dwarf conifer, very compact with deep green, glossy foliage quite outstanding in spring when making new growth. **Ideal in a conifer bed** or rockery where after thirty or forty years time it may be only 3 ft. high and 2 ft. wide.

Abies koreana

A beautiful small conifer with a neat conical habit. The foliage is glossy green on top, whitish beneath. Cones appear at an early age and are purple, pointing upwards.

Abies lasiocarpa 'Compacta'

A slow growing form of the Alpine Fir with an irregular shape. Particularly attractive when the fresh growth appears in May and June. An ideal conifer for a heather garden or large rockery and an alternative to Picea pungens globosa.

Abies procera 'Glauca Prostrata'

A gem of a plant with bright blue foliage. The cones are very attractive in spring. Ideal with heathers and other dwarf conifers.

Abutilon vitifolium

A large, handsome shrub needing a sunny, sheltered site. Saucer shaped flowers like a single Hollyhock, pale to deep mauve from May to July. The handsome vine shaped leaves are grey and downy. Not a long lived shrub but it produces seeds so profusely that it is easy to maintain stock. Introduced from Chile in 1836.

Acer griseum

One of the most striking of the Maples and a lovely tree for the small garden. The trifoliate leaves colour beautifully to red and orange in the autumn. In addition the old bark on the trunk and the main branches peels in to large flakes to reveal the cinnaman coloured underbark. Rare in cultivation because of the low germination rate (5%) of its seeds. Award of Garden Merit 1936. Introduction from Central China in 1901.

Acer japonicum 'Aconitifolium' (Laciniatum)

If you want a shrub for brilliant autumn colour, go no further, once established, this is fantastic, its deeply cut leaves turn rich ruby crimson in autumn. Makes a rounded shrub and eventually a small tree. Award of Garden Merit 1957.

Acer negundo 'Flamingo'

A recent introduction, which can be grown as a shrub or a small tree. A selected form of A. negundo with the young leaves opening light pink, changing as they mature to green with white variegation. Can be lightly pruned to shape and the lady of the house may assist in this 'pruning' for floral decoration. Will make a lovely specimen tree and enjoys full sun or semi shade.

Acer palmatum

This Japanese Maple is an outstanding shrub or small tree with its leaves bright green all summer, turning brilliant orange crimson in autumn. Can be planted in small or large gardens. Award of Garden Merit 1969.

Acer palmatum 'Aureum'

This real gem of a plant needs time to establish, as in its early days its lovely golden foliage is apt to scorch. But it is worth the waiting as its butter yellow foliage and slow growing habit are quite outstanding.

Acer palmatum 'Bloodgood'

A superb variety of Japanese maple with rich red purple foliage that is outstanding in a sunny position as it highlights the colour. A lovely specimen shrub for the lawn.

Acer palmatum 'Dissectum Atropurpureum'

One of the most popular of the Japanese Maples, its mushroom shape and finely cut purple red foliage make it a real beauty. Needs a sheltered position away from east winds. May take a little time to look at its best,but worth the wait. Award of Garden Merit 1928.

Acer palmatum 'Dissectum'

One of the real gems of the garden. A slow growing mushroom shaped shrub with finely divided green leaves all summer and gorgeous autumn colours. Needs a sheltered position away from east winds. Ideal planted with conifers or shrubs. Award of Garden Merit 1956.

Acer palmatum 'Heptalobum Osakazuki'

Probably the most brilliant Japanese Maple for autumn colour, when the green leaves turn to fiery scarlet and orange. It makes a handsome specimen tree. Award of Merit 1969.

Acer palmatum 'Senkaki'

An outstanding Japanese Maple for summer and winter beauty. The attractivelight green maple leaves turn butter yellow in autumn. The branches are bright red, resembling Dogwood and providing valuable winter colour. Award of Garden Merit 1969. Introduced by Sunningdale Nurseries in 1920.

Acer palmatum Atropurpureum

Always a very popular Japanese Maple with crimson purple foliage throughout the summer. The leaves are typical in shape and five lobed, sometimes partly seven-lobed. **Excellent as a specimen** in a lawn and in the shrubbery. Award of Garden merit. 1928.

Acer palmatum dissectum 'Crimson Queen'

A selected clone of A. p. dissectum atropurpureum. The dissectum group are generally shrubby in form, making a mushroom shaped bush when young . The leaves are finely and delicately cut, giving a feathery appearance. Rich plum purple foliage throughout the summer. In the autumn they become a bright orange red before leaf-fall. Purple stems are a winter feature. A most desirable plant for the rock garden or near a pool.

Agave americana 'Mediopicta'

A striking succulent plant, consisting mainly of a rosette of greyish sword-like leaves with a central cream stripe. The leaves are 10 to 12 ins. long. Called 'Century Plant' because it is incorrectly said not to flower until it is 100 years old. 'Half Century' would be more accurate. When it does flower, the inflorescence is up to 25 ft. tall with white flowers. **A good container plant for the patio or conservatory**, it needs exceptionally well drained soil and a sheltered spot.

Amelanchier canadensis (Lamarckii)

A medium sized deciduous shrub, thriving on moist lime free soil. In the spring the white flowers are borne in groups of eight to ten, followed by purple-black berries. In the autumn the leaves are richly coloured in tints of red and orange. We have retained the specific epithet 'canadensis' but this plant is correctly A.lamarckii since 1941. It has also been variously wrongly named A. x grandiflora, A. laevis and confusa. It has been cultivated in our gardens since the early 1800's.

Andromeda polifolia 'Compacta'

This is a charming dwarf shrub for the peat bed or cool peaty area. It is evergreen, bearing bright pink flowers, in May and June, in short compact clusters at the end of the shoots. The leaves are dark green above and glaucous or slightly felty beneath. Native of the colder parts of the Northern Hemisphere.

Aralia elata 'Aureovariegata'

This rather surprisingly little known shrub or small tree is grown for its handsome foliage, splashed yellow on the large pinnate leaves. Flowers, white in large panicles from July to September. At its best in a sheltered position in the colder parts of the country. **Possibly one of the most beautiful and effective of all variegated shrubs**.

Aralia elata 'Variegata'

This little known shrub / small tree should be more widely planted. Its large pinnate leaves are irregularly margined and blotched creamy white. Whiteflowers in large panicles appear from July to September. At its best in a sheltered position in the colder parts of the country.

Araucaria araucana

A very unusual conifer with thick, dark green branches. The leaves are arranged in spirals along the length of the branch. **Slow growing** but in time will make a large tree.

Arbutus unedo

An attractive, hardy evergreen with dark, glossy foliage and strawberry shaped fruits in late autumn. A native of the Mediterranean and South West Ireland. As the plant ages it sheds its dark brown bark, adding to the interest, The fruit ripens in the autumn following the production of the flowers at the same time as the succeeding crop of blossom is opening.

Aronia arbutifolia

An attractive medium sized shrub with interest from spring to autumn: white flowers about half an inch across in spring followed by red berries and brilliant autumn colours of yellow, red and orange. Closely related to the Mountain Ash and introduced from North America about 1700.

Artemesia absinthium 'Lambrook silver'

A form selected by Margery Fish and named after her home Lambrook Manor, making a shimmer of silky grey much divided leaves. The flowers are tiny yellowish in colour and carried in much branched spikes. It makes a perfect contrast with purple leaved shrubs and needs a warm well drained position. Must be pruned in late spring to retain compactness.

Arundinaria japonica

An extremely adaptable and hardy bamboo, forming dense thickets of olive green canes up to 18 ft. high, arching at the top, bearing lush masses of dark green, glossy leaves. Only very occasionally produces flowers (said to be once every 100 years).

Arundinaria murieliae

This graceful bamboo makes a fine specimen plant, and can also be grown in a tub. The canes are bright green at first, maturing to yellow green. The foliage is bright pea green.

Arundinaria nitida

An elegant bamboo forming graceful arching clumps 9-11 ft. high, with purple flushed canes. Can be grown as a specimen plant or in a large tub.

Arundinaria pygmaea

This dwarf bamboo makes **excellent ground cover**, forming a carpet of slender stems.

Arundinaria viridistriata (auricoma)

A colourful bamboo with green leaves striped yellow. If grown in shade, it keeps lower growth than if grown in sun. Makes a nice tub specimen.

Aucuba japonica 'Crotonifolia' (Crotonoides)

This plant is considered the most beautiful of the spotted laurels. The leaves are green with bold splashes of bright yellow, resembling those of the indoor plant 'Croton' or "Joseph's Coat". It is a very tolerant plant and will stand quite adverse conditions. As well as being an ornamental plant, it is also useful for pollinating the female forms eg 'Variegata'.

Aucuba japonica 'Picturata'

A male form of the 'spotted Laurel' and perhaps the most definitely variegated of all, having broad and solid yellow patches on a mid green background. An excellent pollinator for Aucuba jap. Variegata. The Aucubas more than any other evergreen are able to tolerate dense shade and remain cheerful.

Aucuba japonica 'Speckles'

The spotted laurel is one of the easiest plants to please, and will tolerate dense shade. It has green leaves speckled with white and a compact, rounded habit. This is a male form of aucuba, which will set berries on the female forms.

Aucuba japonica 'Variegata'

This easy to please shrub can be grown in dense shade or full sun. The leaves are green, speckled with yellow. This is a female form of aucuba that will bear red berries in autumn if a male form is nearby, ie. A. jap. Speckles, Crotonoides or Picturata. The Aucubas more than any other evergreen are able to tolerate shade and remain cheerful. They will even grow where grass will not and their roots fight against those of its big neighbours.

Azalea Knap Hill 'Brazil'

A superb shrub with bright tangerine red flowers that darken with age, the petal margins are attractively frilled. The foliage turns lovely colours in autumn.

Azalea Knap Hill 'Gibraltar'

A superb variety, the large, flame orange flowers have a yellow flash and crinkly petals. The buds are deep crimson orange.

Azalea Knap Hill 'Glowing Embers'

A very colourful variety. The flowers are trumpet shaped, reddish orange with a yellow blotch. Good autumn foliage.

Azalea Knap Hill 'Gog'

The orange red flowers have a yellow flash and are flushed dark red on the outside.

Azalea Knap Hill 'Homebush'

A colourful shrub with tight heads of semi double, rose pink flowers with paler shading. The foliage has good autumn colour.

Azalea Knap Hill 'Kathleen'

A very colourful shrub with salmon pink, orange blotched flowers. The buds are darker. The foliage has rich autumn tints.

Azalea Knap Hill 'Satan'

One of the Knaphill cultivars with geranium-red flowers, darker in bud.

Azalea Knap Hill 'Silver Slipper'

A superb and colourful shrub with white flushed pink flowers, and orange flare. Young foliage has a copper tint.

Azalea Knap Hill 'Whitethroat'

A beautiful cultivar, the blooms are double, pure white with frilly margins, appearing in May. The habit is compact and the foliage often tints well in autumn.

Azalea japonica (General)

The evergreen azaleas are free flowering and compact growing members of the genus Rhododendron. The term Japanese correctly refers to the 50 varieties introduced by E. H. Wilson in 1918, since when much hybridising has been and still is being carried out in Holland and the U.S.A. They make excellent tub specimens. The colour range is white through red and pink to crimson and purple. They must be planted in acid soil.

Azalea japonica 'Achgadir'

A useful and decorative small shrub. The glossy, evergreen leaves set off the bright red flowers, which appear in late April and May in great numbers. Good for tubs and the rock garden.

Azalea japonica 'Aladdin'

A fine evergreen shrub with small glossy leaves and masses of red flowers in May. **Excellent when planted with dwarf conifers and heathers**.

Azalea japonica 'Amoena'

A dwarf evergreen, making excellent ground cover in lightly shaded areas. Masses of purplish red flowers appear in May. Enjoys peaty soil.

Azalea japonica 'Arendsii'

A small evergreen shrub with glossy green leaves. Pale purple flowers with a sprinkling of red spots, appear in April or May. **The habit is low and spreading**.

Azalea japonica 'Blaauws Pink'

This is one of the best known Japanese Azaleas. It has a slightly upright habit, shiny evergreen foliage and salmon pink flowers with paler shading.

Azalea japonica 'Blue Danube'

A small japanese azalea with a spreading habit. The foliage is glossy green, and the flowers, which are quite large, are an unusual shade of violet blue. May be grown on a rock garden.

Azalea japonica 'Esmeralda'

A charming dwarf evergreen azalea with many pale pink, hose in hose flowers. Introduced by Koppeschaar of Boskoop, Holland.

Azalea japonica 'Excelsior'

An upright growing azalea with glossy, evergreen foliage that turns deep purple in winter. Bright red flowers in great numbers, appear in spring. A good tub plant which looks attractive even when not in flower.

Azalea japonica 'Favorite'

A small evergreen shrub with deep rosy pink flowers. Ideal in groups with Rhododendrons and peat loving plants. Its low, compact habit makes it an ideal tub plant.

Azalea japonica 'Fedora'

A lovely evergreen shrub, compact and small. Pale pink, darker flashed flowers appear in May, often covering the plant in blooms.

Azalea japonica 'Gretchen'

A small evergreen shrub of upright habit with quite large, deep mauve flowers. Ideal to plant in front of larger shrubs etc. as long as it has lime free soil and is not allowed to dry out.

Azalea japonica 'Hatsugiri'

A very small, compact, evergreen azalea with crimson purple flowers in April and May. Peaty conditions and semi shade are ideal. The foliage often tints red in autumn.

Azalea japonica 'Hino Crimson'

A compact growing dwarf evergreen, producing masses of red flowers in April and May. Peaty conditions and semi shade are ideal. The foliage often tints red in autumn.

Azalea japonica 'Ima-Shojo'

A lovely evergreen Kurume Azalea with bright red, hose in hose flowers and good foliage. One of the E.H. Wilson's original 50 introduced in 1918 from a selection at the Akashi Nursery, Japan (Wilson No 36 Fascination). Very hardy and compact growing to form a small mound.

Azalea japonica 'Kermissine'

A compact evergren azalea. Masses of carmine flowers appear in April and May, almost covering the plant.

Azalea japonica 'Lilli Marlene'

An evergreen Azalea which has vigorous and up right habit. Very free flowering double, hose to hose rose-red blooms in compact trusses. Award of Merit 1982.

Azalea japonica 'Mikador'

A small evergreen shrub producing masses of pink flowers in spring. The foliage is glossy green, turning dark purple in winter. Good for tubs and on the rockery.

Azalea japonica 'Mother's Day'

A charming dwarf evergreen with masses of red flowers in April and May. Ideal in sheltered, semi shaded position.

Azalea japonica 'Orange Beauty'

A popular, dwarf evergreen azalea of upright habit, with salmon orange flowers in May and June. **Peaty conditions and semi shade are ideal**. The foliage often tints red in autumn.

Azalea japonica 'Palestrina'

An unusual and upright growing azalea. The white flowers have a faint green ray inside, and appear in April and May. Good for tubs and on rockeries.

Azalea japonica 'Red Pimpernel'

A colourful, dwarf evergreen azalea with orange red flowers. Ideal for underplanting of larger shrubs.

Azalea japonica 'Rose Bud'

A superb Azalea with clear pink flowers and low spreading habit. This variety can be forced in to early flowering and is often sold as a winter pot plant. **Very good in the small garden**.

Azalea japonica 'Silvester'

A compact growing, evergreen azalea producing its rosy red flowers slightly earlier than most of the Japanese azaleas. Peaty conditions and semi shade are ideal. The foliage often tints red in autumn.

Azalea japonica 'Thierry'

A compact, evergreen azalea, one of the smaller varieties. Masses of small, orangey red flowers appear in April, May. The foliage turns deep purple in autumn. Good for tubs and on a rockery.

Azalea japonica 'Vuyk's Rosyred'

A compact growing, evergreen azalea. The deep rose flowers appear in spring and have a dark flash. Peaty conditions and semi shade are ideal. The foliage often tints red in autumn.

Azalea japonica 'Vuyk's Scarlet'

A compact growing, evergreen azalea with bright red, wavy edged petals. Peaty conditions and semi shade are ideal. The foliage often tints red in autumn.

Azalea mollis 'Hortulanus H. Witte'

A very colourful shrub producing bright, orange yellow flowers in early May, before the leaves. Good autumn colour. **Always best planted in sun or semi shade and peaty soil**.

Azalea mollis 'Koningin Emma'

A very colourful shrub, producing its orange flowers in early May before the foliage. Ideal for planting with Rhododendrons, and heathers. The foliage often tints red in autumn.

Azalea mollis 'Koster's Brilliant Red'

A superb deciduous azalea with glowing, orange red flowers. The foliage turns red and orange in autumn.

Azalea mollis 'Mathilda'

A very colourful shrub producing orange red, trumpet shaped flowers in early May. Good autumn colour. Always best planted in peaty soil. Ideal with rhododendrons etc.

Azalea mollis Standard form.

An outstanding shrub, grown as a half standard on a three foot stem using various cultivars, in colours of red, yellow and orange. Valuable for giving immediate height to a planting area.

Azalea mollis mixed colours

Lovely deciduous shrubs, the flower colours range from yellow, red and orange and they very often produce good autumn colours.

Berberis 'Parkjuweel'

A small semi evergreen shrub of dense, prickly habit. Small, pale yellow flowers appear in spring, but this plant is mainly grown for its brilliant autumn colours.

Berberis buxifolia 'Nana'

A dwarf, evergreen shrub with yellow flowers when planted in open position. The foliage turns deep red in winter. Ideal for the rock garden or shrub border. **Makes a very good dwarf hedge**.

Berberis candidula

A dense growing, dome shaped bush with small, dark green, prickly leaves,silver beneath. Yellow flowers appear in spring, followed by blue blackberries in autumn.

Berberis darwinii

One of the finest evergreen, spring flowering shrubs, with strong yellow flowers followed by blue berries. Glossy, dark green foliage and evergreen. Can be used as an informal hedge as well as in a shrubbery. Discovered by Darwin on the voyage of the "Beagle' and introduced in 1849 by Messrs Veitch.

Berberis julianae

An excellent evergreen shrub with strong, spiny stems and clusters of stiff, narrow, spine toothed leaves, copper tinted when young. Slightly scented yellow flowers appear in spring. **A useful hedging and screening plant**.

Berberis linearifolia 'Orange King'

Considered by some to be the best of the evergreen barberries. The type was introduced from Chile in 1927. This selected form has rich orange flowers. The leaves are long and toothless unlike B.darwinii. The plant makes an erect shrub of loose habit 5-8ft. in height and would make an excellent informal hedge.

Berberis thunbergii

An outstanding small shrub, compact in growth with yellow flowers followed by red berries. Unsurpassed in the brilliance of its autumn foliage. Makes an excellent hedging plant.

Berberis thunbergii 'Atropurpurea Nana'

A charming shrub with reddish purple foliage all summer and yellow flowers in spring. Suitable for shrubbery or rock garden. **Ideal dwarf hedge**.

Berberis thunbergii 'Atropurpurea'

A small shrub of great value for its compact habit and bright red foliage all summer, increasing in intensity as winter approaches. Also bears yellow flowers in spring followed by red berries. **Makes a good hedging plant**.

Berberis thunbergii 'Aurea'

A small shrub with very bright yellow foliage in early summer which turns to pale green in late summer, also good autumn colour. Best planted in semi shade as the yellow foliage colour lasts longer. **May scorch in full sun**.

Berberis thunbergii 'Harlequin'

This barberry is another selected clone, similar to B. thun. Rose Glow but with even more pronounced variegation. The leaves are heavily marbled cream and deep pink. The young growth has coral red stems and a gold tinge to the leaves. A very desirable medium sized shrub and would make an interesting hedge.

Berberis thunbergii 'Helmond Pillar'

A new variety. It is one of the only really fastigiate ,red leaved shrubs. A very worthwhile addition to the garden.

Berberis thunbergii 'Rose Glow'

This is one of my favourite shrubs, very striking, small, with leaves of the young shoots purple, mottled silver pink and bright rose, later becoming purple. Yellow flowers in spring. Not often used for hedging,but well worth a try.

Berberis verruculosa

A slow growing evergreen shrub from China with a compact habit. Golden yellow flowers appear in May and June followed by black berries.

Berberis wilsoniae

Another one of the splendid shrubs first found in China. It forms a dense mound of sea green foliage with pale yellow flowers in spring, followed by coral red berries which blend with the attractive foliage tints in autumn.

Berberis x lologensis 'Apricot Queen'

A lovely hybrid from B. darwinii x B. linearifolia, with apricot-yellow flowers. The evergreen foliage is inherited from the darwinii parent. These plants have been found to do well on chalk. Discovered in Argentina in 1927.

Berberis x ottawensis 'Gold Ring'

A new variety of Berberis that looks to be quite outstanding. The habit is compact with maroon leaves that have a narrow gold band round the edge. Yellow flowers appear in spring. A highly recommended form that would make an interesting hedge.

Berberis x ottawensis 'Purpruea'

This outstanding red/purple leaved shrub is quite startling all summer, contrasting well with green and blue shrubs. Yellow flowers in spring are followed by red berries.

Berberis x stenophylla

A hybrid which first appeared about 1860. The bush forms a mass of branches from which it throws arching shoots 1 foot or more long. The following year these are wreathed from end to end with rich golden-yellow flowers. When well grown it is one of the loveliest spring flowering shrubs. It is excellent in the shrubbery or as a lawn specimen and it makes an excellent informal hedge. Prune each year after flowering.

Buddleia 'Lochinch'

A bushy, compact shrub with handsome greyish young stems, and leaves with white undersides. Scented, violet blue flowers, each with an orange eye, appear from July to Sept.
A hybrid between B.davidii and B.fallowiana.

Buddleia alternifolia

A splendid and very graceful shrub with narrow green leaves, wreathed in delicately fragrant, lilac flowers in June.

Buddleia davidii 'Black Knight'

One of the most widely planted shrubs. Long trusses of very deep violet, fragrant flowers. Like all buddleias, attracts butterflies. Plant in a sunny spot. **Best results obtained if pruned hard in March.**

Buddleia davidii 'Border Beauty'

This is a more compact variety of Buddleia with deep crimson purple, fragrant flowers in summer and early autumn.

Buddleia davidii 'Empire Blue'

A widely planted shrub with rich, violet blue flowers with orange eyes. These fragrant flowers attract the butterflies. Best results obtained if pruned hard in March.

Buddleia davidii 'Fascination'

An outstanding, summer flowering shrub, producing wide, full panicles of vivid, lilac pink, fragrant flowers from July to September. Best results obtained if pruned hard in March.

Buddleia davidii 'Harlequin'

A variegated form of the 'Butterfly Bush' with attractive, yellow edged leaves. Rich red purple flowers appear from July to September. This form is a 'sport' of Buddleia 'Royal Red".

Buddleia davidii 'Ile de France'

A fine, summer flowering shrub, producing rich, violet racemes from July to September. Best results obtained if pruned hard in March.

Buddleia davidii 'Nanho Blue'

A form of Buddleia d. nanhoensis with blue flowers and smaller in all its parts than most of the 'davidii' cultivars, making it an ideal 'Butterfly Bush' for the smaller garden. Must be hard pruned each March and needs a position in full sun.

Buddleia davidii 'Royal Red'

An outstanding variety of the butterfly bush, with massive panicles of red purple flowers from July to September. Best results obtained if pruned hard in March.

Buddleia davidii 'White Bouquet'

A fine tall summer flowering shrub producing large panicles of fragrant white, yellow eyed flowers from July to September. Should be hard pruned in March for best results.

Buddleia davidii 'White Cloud'

The name of this butterfly bush speaks for itself, pure white, dense panicles of flowers from July to September. Best results obtained if pruned hard in March.

Buddleia davidii 'White Profusion'

A beautiful variety of the Butterfly Bush with long panicles of white flowers, each with a yellow eye. All varieties of this shrub are very attractive to bees and butterflies.

Buddleia globosa

A striking evergreen shrub of upright habit with handsome foliage. Scented, orange yellow, ball like flowers appear in May and June.

Buxus sempervirens

This slow growing evergreen is mostly used as dwarf hedging, as it is very neat in growth and if needed, could be kept as low as 6". It is also used for topiary.

Buxus sempervirens 'Elegantissima'

An attractive slow growing evergreen with small leaves edged with creamy white. Makes a very good dwarf hedge as well as specimen shrub.

Callicarpa bodinieri 'Profusion'

Not planted as often as it should be. Lilac flowers in late summer are followed by deep lilac fruits in clusters, which can last to late December. **Autumn colour is quite outstanding**.

Callistemon linearis

A delightful evergreen shrub which requires the protection of a South or South - West facing wall. The red flowers are borne in dense spikes resembling a bottle brush in July - August. **Excellent as a conservatory plant**.

Calluna vulgaris cultivars

These are summer flowering heathers, known to all who have lived or travelled in Britain. They are very variable plants and scores of varieties have been identified and named, many of them valuable for their foliage colour, of greens, gold and bronze.

Calluna vulgaris 'Alba Plena'

A superb plant that often starts with single white flowers, before the double flowers in long sprays appear. The habit is rather prostrate and spreading with pale to dark green foliage.

Calluna vulgaris 'Alba Rigida'

Forms a tight, low growing plant with bright green foliage bearing short compact sprays of white flowers.

Calluna vulgaris 'Allegro'

A new variety of heather that has one of the deepest red flowers in the calluna range. The foliage is a deep green.

Calluna vulgaris 'Alportii'

The crimson flowers are borne on strong spikes, the growth is vigorous and will soon form a large, upright plant with dark green foliage.

Calluna vulgaris 'Beoley Gold'

This is a strong sturdy grower with single, pure white flowers in short sprays. The foliage is a bright golden yellow.

Calluna vulgaris 'Blazeaway'

A tall and upright plant with light mauve flowers. The foliage is a pale yellow green with deep orange tints, turning to brilliant red in winter on exposed surfaces of the plant.

Calluna vulgaris 'Bonfire Brilliance'

A fast growing heather with an upright habit. The foliage is brilliant yellow, orange and scarlet, the colours intensifying in winter. The flowers are a soft lilac.

Calluna vulgaris 'Boskoop'

A most impressive plant with rich gold foliage that becomes orange red in hard weather. The flowers are lilac rose on tapering spikes.

Calluna vulgaris 'County Wicklow'

One of the finest heathers, suitable for even the smallest garden. The foliage is light green, darkening in winter. The flowers are soft pink and borne in rather short, closely packed spikes.

Calluna vulgaris 'Cuprea'

Although an old cultivar, this is still one of the best and most popular. The plant is slender and upright with lilac flowers. The foliage is yellow with coppery tones, turning to bronzed red in winter.

Calluna vulgaris 'Darkness'

Regarded as one of the finest heathers when compared with those of similar colouring, both for neat compact growth and the prolific amount of bloom. The foliage is soft bright green and the flowers bright crimson, tinged with purple.

Calluna vulgaris 'Drum-Ra'

A taller plant with rather stiffer branches, varying in height and bearing white flowers. The foliage has a fresh green colour.

Calluna vulgaris 'Elsie Purnell'

A well grown plant presents a magnificent sight, with its silver green foliage and the flowers, soft rose with white centres in solid, very long spikes.

Calluna vulgaris 'Gold Haze'

The foliage is a clear golden yellow, the flowers are white, single and borne in long sprays.

Calluna vulgaris 'Golden Carpet'

A prostrate plant that eventually forms a low hummock. The flowers are purple, borne on short spikes with yellow foliage that shows orange tints in the winter.

Calluna vulgaris 'Golden Feather'

The foliage is a soft yellow, flushed orange, on long feather like plumes which are sometimes tinged deep orange and red in winter. Rather prostrate in the first season, becoming more vigorous and spreading.

Calluna vulgaris 'H.E. Beale'

A vigorous plant which, if well cultivated, will provide a wonderful display for many years. The foliage is grey green with long sprays of pale, silvery pink flowers.

Calluna vulgaris 'Hammondii'

One of the oldest heathers in cultivation yet still regarded as one of the best 'whites'. The foliage is a rich green, the flowers are borne in long solid spikes.

Calluna vulgaris 'J.H. Hamilton'

The foliage is dark green with clear, bright pink flowers in dainty sprays. A compact grower that does well in heavy soils. **The cut stems last well when dried** and used for winter decoration in vases.

Calluna vulgaris 'John F. Letts'

Prostrate and low growing, it makes a perfect plant for a bright splash of colour on the winter rockery. The foliage is a light yellow gold, flecked with orange and red, the colours intensifying in cold weather. The flowers are pale lavender on small stems.

Calluna vulgaris 'Joy Vanstone'

The pale lilac mauve flowers in long sprays provide a pleasing contrast with the foliage, which is pale gold with a hint of orange towards autumn. The winter colour is bright gold with deep orange shades, sometimes banded in red.

Calluna vulgaris 'Kinlochruel'

The flowers are fully double, white, open wide and borne on short stems. The foliage is deep green, becoming purplish green in winter.

Calluna vulgaris 'Multicolor'

A compact, low and bushy plant with mauve flowers borne on short spikes. The foliage is pale orange yellow, turning deeper orange red. The winter colour varies from red to dark purple.

Calluna vulgaris 'Orange Queen'

This plant has an upright habit with foliage that is pale yellow, becoming soft orange with deeper coloured tips. The flowers are mauve in strong spikes.

Calluna vulgaris 'Peter Sparkes'

The flowers are deep pink in strong spikes. A beautiful form in which the fully double florets are also carried on short laterals at the base of the main spike. The foliage is a dark grey green.

Calluna vulgaris 'Ralph Purnell'

An imposing plant, the flowers are reddish purple on strong upright spikes, and make excellent cut flowers. The foliage is a dull green.

Calluna vulgaris 'Robert Chapman'

The foliage is greenish yellow with orange red tints. During autumn the orange intensifies, and winter colour is brilliant red where exposed to the frost and sun. The flowers are bright mauve pink and the plant has an upright, compact habit.

Calluna vulgaris 'Ruth Sparkes'

A compact, spreading plant with white double flowers in long sprays. The foliage is bright golden yellow, especially in the winter.

Calluna vulgaris 'Serlei Aurea'

The foliage is a soft, feathery pale yellow, deepening to gold in the winter. The flowers are single and white.

Calluna vulgaris 'Silver Queen'

An exquisite plant. The foliage is green, but completely overlaid with fine white hairs to give a grey or silver blue effect. The flowers are pinkish lavender, generously produced in long sprays.

Calluna vulgaris 'Silver Rose'

The charm of this heather lies in the abundance of slender, tapering flower stems, bearing silver rose pink flowers, well displayed against the soft, hairy, silver green leaves.

Calluna vulgaris 'Sir John Charrington'

A plant with beautiful flowers and foliage. The flowers are a distinctive, deep maroon purple on long graceful spikes, whilst the foliage is pale yellow - gold shaded orange with deeper orange tints in summer. In winter the colour intensifies.

Calluna vulgaris 'Sister Anne'

A plant of dense and compact habit, with soft, thick greyish green foliage. Pink flowers are produced in great profusion.

Calluna vulgaris 'Sunrise'

This plant has spectacular foliage, bright gold in summer changing through orange to a brilliant red in winter. The mauve flowers are borne in long spikes.

Calluna vulgaris 'Sunset'

The foliage is pale yellow with orange and red tints, becoming bright red in winter. The pale pink flowers are borne on short sprays.

Calluna vulgaris 'Underwoodii'

A plant with delicate, upright growth of medium height and mid green foliage. The flowers are a haze of silver pink buds which never open.

Calluna vulgaris 'White Lawn'

A small and compact plant with rich green foliage. The small white flowers are borne on short spikes.

Calluna vulgaris 'Winter Chocolate'

A plant with beautiful foliage that is greenish yellow and orange, becoming golden yellow with orange tips, finally dark chocolate with red tips. The flowers are a lilac pink.

Camellia japonica 'Alba Simplex'

An outstanding evergreen with rich green, glossy foliage. White single flowers with conspicuous stamens are normally produced from February to May, depending on growing conditions and season.

Camellia japonica 'Billie McFarland'

A superb evergreen shrub with glossy, deep green foliage. Pink, single flowers with yellow stamens open in late winter. A good tub specimen.

Camellia japonica 'Blood of China'

A fine evergreen with rich green, glossy foliage and deep, salmon red, semi double flowers, produced between February and May, depending on growing conditions and season.

Camellia japonica 'Bobs Tinsie'

A very unusual looking camellia with red flowers, each with a tight mound of very short petals in its centre. The leaves are deep green and glossy. A good tub plant.

Camellia japonica 'Brigadoon'

An evergreen, late winter flowering shrub. The flowers are semi-double and of a delicate shade of pink. Flowers appear from February to April, depending on climate. A good plant for growing in a tub.

Camellia japonica 'Brushfields Yellow'

A striking hybrid with an outer white ring of petals, surrounding an inner cluster of short yellow petals. A good tub plant.

Camellia japonica 'Dainty'

A superb evergreen with rich, glossy green foliage. The flower is very unusual, white with blotches and stripes of red with yellow stamens.

Camellia japonica 'Diamond Head'

A very pretty camellia, the flowers are semi-double, a rich pink, appearing in late winter when colour is badly needed. The evergreen foliage is a feature, also its suitability for tubs.

Camellia japonica 'El Dorado'

A superb evergreen shrub, the bright green glossy foliage sets off the double, salmon coloured flowers.

Camellia japonica 'Elegans'

A fine evergreen with rich green, glossy foliage and deep pink, double flowers appearing between February and April depending on growing conditions and season.

Camellia japonica 'Flame'

This evergreen shrub makes a fine display in late winter with its semi-double, bright flame red flowers. A good tub specimen.

Camellia japonica 'Grand Prix'

A useful evergreen shrub. Bright orange red flowers with a cluster of stamens, appear in late winter as a valuable splash of colour. A good plant for tubs.

Camellia japonica 'Guest of Honour'

A lovely evergreen with glossy foliage and large, semi double, salmon pink flowers. The growth is compact and upright.

Camellia japonica 'Guillio Nuccio'

An evergreen shrub with semi double, pinky red flowers, each with a yellow centre. Deep glossy green foliage. **Ideal plant for a tub**.

Camellia japonica 'Jury's Yellow'

Not a true yellow, but the yellow petaloids at the anemone centre of the flower reflect their colour onto the white of the surrounding petals. Flowers early in its life and is more resistant to the weather than other 'yellows'.

Camellia japonica 'Kick Off'

An unusual looking camellia with 'paeony form' flowers, the blooms are salmon, with delicate brush strokes of a deeper shade. A good tub plant.

Camellia japonica 'Kitty'

An outstanding evergreen with bright glossy green foliage. The flower is yellow in the centre, creamy white with a pink blush on the outside of the petals.

Camellia japonica 'Lady Clare'

A superb evergreen with rich glossy foliage and semi double, clear pink flowers, appearing from February to April depending on growing conditions and season.

Camellia japonica 'Laura Walker'

A semi double camellia with deep pink flowers. Yellow stamens appear between short inner petals. Good for tubs, glossy evergreen foliage.

Camellia japonica 'Margaret Davies'

A paeony form camellia, the petals are short in the centre of the flower, the yellow stamens peeping out from in between. Attractive evergreen foliage.

Camellia japonica 'Mary Phoebe Taylor'

A lovely evergreen shrub with pink semi double flowers early in the year. The foliage is rich green. An ideal plant for tubs.

Camellia japonica 'Powder Puff'

A lovely white Camellia with white paeony form flowers 2' to 4' in diameter held on a medium sized bush of compact habit. Introduced in U.S.A. in 1960 and flowering in mid-season. Excellent for a tub.

Camellia japonica 'Red Ensign'

A valuable shrub for colour early in the year. The glossy, deep green foliage sets off the bright scarlet, semi-double flowers, each with a central cluster of yellow stamens. A very good plant to grow in a tub.

Camellia japonica 'Shirobotan'

A very beautiful evergreen, which produces white flowers with yellow stamens, during late winter.

Camellia japonica 'The Czar'

A superb evergreen shrub with light red, semi-double, quite flat flowers, each with a prominent cluster of tight yellow stamens. A plant that provides valuable late winter colour, and may also be grown in a tub.

Camellia sasanqua 'Yuletide'

A very early flowering camellia. The bright red, single flowers with prominent stamens, appear from November to February. The foliage is evergreen and the plant may also be grown in a tub.

Camellia x williamsii 'Anticipation'

A fairly recent introduction from New Zealand. The deep green, evergreen foliage sets off the large, double, deep crimson flowers. A good subject for tubs.

Camellia x williamsii 'Ballet Queen'

A semi double, paeony form camellia with mid pink flowers in late winter. The glossy green foliage sets the flowers off well and makes a feature of the plant all year. **Good for tubs**.

Camellia x williamsii 'Barbara Clark'

A Saluensis/reticulata hybrid with semi-double rose pink, medium size flowers which are long lasting.

Camellia x williamsii 'Daintiness'

Semi-double, long lasting flowers, rose pink with cream stamens. Excellent under glass early on but perfectly hardy for out-doors. The bush is open and graceful. **Camellias should never be planted where their flowers can receive the morning sun**.

Camellia x williamsii 'Debbie'

A new hybrid from New Zealand. The flowers are 'paeony form' which means that they have an outer ring of petals with a cluster of shorter petals in the centre. The colour is a clear pink and flowers may appear from March to April. **All camellias make good tub plants, for patios, balconies etc**.

Camellia x williamsii 'Donation'

One of the most beautiful camellias with its rich glossy foliage and large, orchid pink, semi double flowers from February to April depending on growing conditions and season.

Camellia x williamsii 'Elegant Beauty'

A beautiful shrub with salmon orange, semi-double flowers with yellow stamens. Flowering takes place in late winter, providing much needed colour. This plant may also be grown in a tub.

Camellia x williamsii 'Shocking pink'

A beautiful form of camellia with semi double, bright pink flowers early in the season. A good tub plant.

Camellia x williamsii 'Waterlily'

A lovely evergreen with delicate pink, semi-double flowers which open in late winter. This plant may also be grown in a tub to great effect.

Caragana arborescens

A deciduous shrub, which by pruning away the lower branches and training a leading shoot may make a small tree up to 15 feet in height. Generally a large shrub with yellow pea-like flowers and small pinnate light green leaves. A native of Siberia and Mongolia, and adapted for growing in very poor soil conditions in full sun. Introduced in 1752.

Caragana arborescens pendula 'Walker'

A recently introduced and improved form of C.arborescens pendula, with stiffly pendant branches, making an attractive small, weeping specimen tree. The pea shaped flowers are yellow as in the type. The small pinnate leaves are nearly hairless and bright green.

Caryopteris x clandonensis

A small late summer and early autumn flowering shrub with aromatic greyish foliage and clusters of bright blue flowers, slightly paler than its named clones such as Arthur Simmonds and Kew Blue.

Caryopteris x clandonensis 'Arthur Simmonds'

A small, late flowering shrub with aromatic leaves and bright blue flowers in August and September. The foliage is silvery grey.

Caryopteris x clandonensis 'Heavenly Blue'

A fine late summer and autumn flowering shrub with narrow, grey green leaves and clusters of blue flowers. The foliage is also aromatic.

Caryopteris x clandonensis 'Kew Blue'

A compact form with rich blue flowers making a valuable display in late summer.

Catalpa bignonioides 'Aurea'

A tree or large shrub with large, heart shaped leaves of golden yellow. White foxglove like flowers appear on mature trees in July and August.

Ceanothus 'A.T. Johnson'

An outstanding, sun loving, evergreen shrub, with rich blue flowers in spring and again in autumn. Best grown against a south facing wall or fence in well drained soil.

Ceanothus 'Autumnal Blue'

One of the hardiest ceanothus. Glossy evergreen foliage sets off clusters of rich blue flowers from summer to autumn. Can be grown against a sunny wall or fence.

Ceanothus 'Burkwoodii'

A much sought after evergreen plant. The flowers are a rich dark blue, appearing in summer and autumn. Ideal for the sheltered town garden.

Ceanothus 'Cascade'

A lovely evergreen hybrid with arching branches and clusters of rich blue flowers in May. Needs a sheltered spot, **good on a sunny wall**.

Ceanothus 'Delight'

A very hardy ceanothus with deep green, evergreen foliage. 2-3 inch long clusters of bright blue flowers appear in May.

Ceanothus 'Gloire de Versailles'

A deciduous ceanothus with large panicles of powder blue flowers in summer and autumn. Unlike other ceanothus can be grown in a more open position, though still needing sun and well drained soil.

Ceanothus 'Puget Blue'

A lovely evergreen with small crinkled leaves. Very deep blue flowers appear in spring. Best grown against a sunny wall.

Ceanothus dentatus

This sun loving, evergreen shrub with bright blue flowers, is best grown against a south facing wall or fence in well drained soil. If you do wish to restrict its growth, prune only previous year's growth and **never prune hard**.

Ceanothus impressus

A very distinct shrub. The small leaves have deeply impressed veins and the flowers are deep blue appearing in spring. Best grown against a sunny wall.

Ceanothus thyrsiflorus repens

A compact, mound forming evergreen with clusters of light blue flowers in May and June. **Good for a large rock garden or on a sunny bank**.

Ceanothus thyrsiflorus repens 'Gnome'

A superb evergreen shrub with rich blue flowers in May and June. Much smaller growing than many of the ceanothus, forming a small mound of rich green foliage. Ideal for the larger rockery or shrub border. **A plantsman's gem**.

Ceanothus x veitchianus

A fine evergreen shrub best planted against a sunny wall with good drainage. Fine rich blue flowers cover the shrub in May and June.

Cedrus atlantica 'Glauca'

One of the most beautiful of all conifers. Rather sparse in its early years, but in time becomes a very imposing tree. Needs space to show its beauty. Stake plants when young to train them up straight.

Cedrus deodara

This tree has a graceful weeping habit. Foliage colour may vary as these plants are grown from seed, some are blue, others are shades of green and grey. **Best given space to show off its beauty**.

Cedrus deodara 'Aurea'

This beautiful weeping conifer is more suited to the small garden than Cedrus Deodara, as it is much slower growing. Its weeping branches are golden yellow in spring and summer, dulling slightly in winter. **Makes a fine lawn specimen**.

Cedrus deodara 'Golden Horizon'

A slow growing conifer almost semi prostrate in habit, with graceful pendulous, golden leaved branches. **Makes excellent ground cover**.

Cedrus libani

This is the familiar flat-topped and tiered cedar of great stature, seen in many historic places. It is slow growing and when young is conical in shape. The foliage is bright to dark green. It was introduced into England from Asia Minor in about 1640.

Cephalanthus occidentalis

An easy to please shrub which produces small, creamy white flowers in August in small, globular heads.

Ceratostigma griffithii

The Ceratostigmas are a small family of plants formerly included in Plumbago which indicates the colour of their flowers. This one is an evergreen plant from the Himalayas with bright blue flowers and bristly leaves which have a reddish tinge in the winter. It is decidedly tender but very desirable and needs a most protected spot and good drainage. It may behave herbaceously in a hard winter.

Ceratostigma plumbaginoides

A quite small shrub suitable for a rock garden or growing in a wall. The small clusters of blue flowers are borne from July to November. The foliage turns red in autumn.

Ceratostigma willmottianum

The hardy plumbago, with its rich blue flowers from July into autumn, and good autumn tints. Best planted in full sun and quite happy once established.

Cercidiphyllum japonicum

This plant can be grown as a small tree or shrub. Valuable for foliage and autumn tints.

Cercis 'Forest Pansy'

A new hybrid with superb, dark purple foliage all summer, new leaves glossy. Pink flowers appear in May, June on established plants but they are rather insignificant beside the magnificent foliage. **Autumn colour is brilliant shades of crimson and red**.

Cercis siliquastrum

A shrub I am surprised is not planted a lot more. Rosy lilac flowers wreath the branches in May, followed by purple tinted seed pods, which are conspicuous from July onwards. Legend says that this is the tree on which Judas hanged himself.

Chaenomeles speciosa 'Nivalis'

An easy to please and tolerant shrub. Still wrongly called 'Japonica' by many. This variety bears large pure white flowers and received an Award of Garden Merit in 1969. Can be trained against a fence or wall, **flowering from February to March**.

Chaenomeles speciosa 'Rubra'

An easy to please shrub with red flowers from late February to March, followed by yellow fruits. Will tolerate poor conditions once established. Can also be used as wall shrub or treated as a normal shrub.

Chaenomeles speciosa 'Sargentii'

A very easy to please shrub, can be trained against a wall or grown as a free standing shrub. Deep red flowers are produced in Feb. and March followed by small quinces.

Chaenomeles x superba 'Boule de Feu'

A hardy shrub of vigorous habit which is closely related to the quince. The flowers are orange red and borne in clusters in spring. The edible fruit which can be used for preserves appears in autumn. Grows well on banks or walls and will tolerate poor conditions once established.

Chaenomeles x superba 'Crimson and Gold'

An outstanding, easy to grow shrub, which many people call Japonica, with deep crimson petals and golden anthers. Flowers any time from February to late March, followed by yellow fruits. Will tolerate poor conditions once established. Can be used as wall shrub or as a normal shrub.

Chaenomeles x superba 'Elly Mossel'

An easy to grow shrub with orange red flowers in late February and March, followed by yellow fruits. Will tolerate poor conditions once established. Can also be used as wall shrub or treated as a normal shrub.

Chaenomeles x superba 'Etna'

A small shrub which is closely related to the quince. The flowers are crimson-scarlet and borne in clusters in spring. The **edible fruit, which can be used for preserves**, appears in autumn. Grows well on banks or walls and will tolerate poor conditions once established.

Chaenomeles x superba 'Fire Dance'

An easy to grow shrub with signal red flowers in March, followed by yellow fruits. Will tolerate poor conditions once established. Can also be used as wall shrub or treated as a normal shrub. Prune after flowering if needed.

Chaenomeles x superba 'Knap Hill Scarlet'

A very tolerant shrub that **provides valuable colour in early spring**. The flowers are bright, orange scarlet, freely produced through spring into early summer. Can be grown as a shrub or against a wall or fence.

Chaenomeles x superba 'Nicoline'

The hybrid Chaenomeles make low spreading shrubs 4 to 5 ft. high and wider across. Nicoline has scarlet red flowers in March followed by edible quice like fruits. The plant can be easily trained to make a handsome wall plant.

Chaenomeles x superba 'Pink Lady'

An easy to grow shrub with clear pink flowers in late February and March, followed by yellow fruits. Will tolerate poor condtions once established. Can also be used as wall shrub or treated as a normal shrub.

Chaenomeles x superba 'Rowallane'

A tough shrub that **will tolerate most conditions of soil and site**. Blood crimson flowers, larger than most, appear in early spring. Can be grown as a shrub or against a wall or fence.

Chaenomeles x superba 'Vermilion'

A tolerant shrub that will make as much of a feature against a wall as it does as a free standing specimen. The flowers are brilliant vermilion, appearing in winter. Edible quinces follow in summer, lasting well into winter.

Chamaecyparis lawsoniana

This conifer was introduced from Oregon and California in 1854, and no other conifer has produced such variety of foliage and form in its seedlings. Many of these have been named and marketed. In its normal form it is a handsome tree with deep green to glaucous green foliage, broadly pyramidal in habit and densely furnished with branches to the ground. Makes a superb evergreen hedge.

Chamaecyparis lawsoniana 'Allumii Gold'

An elegant specimen conifer. The habit is upright with flattened branches tipped a translucent yellow. The colour is brightest during the summer and it should be planted in a sunny location to obtain the best results. May also be used for screening.

Chamaecyparis lawsoniana 'Allumii'

A compact growing conifer with bluish foliage. Makes a good specimen plant and can also be used as screening, though it must not be pruned hard like a Leyland.

Chamaecyparis lawsoniana 'Blue Surprise'

A sport of chamaecyparis Lawsoniana Ellwoodii and one of several having blue-grey foliage. This one is of a deeper blue colour than most and retains semi-juvenile.

Chamaecyparis lawsoniana 'Broomhill Gold'

A very good, compact growing golden conifer. Flame like in shape and requiring a sunny position to do the foliage colour justice. Ideal tub specimen.

Chamaecyparis lawsoniana 'Chilworth Silver'

A very compact, conical conifer, similar to the well known C. 'Ellwoodii' but with much more silvery foliage. Makes an excellent tub specimen and is **very effective planted with heathers and other conifers**.

Chamaecyparis lawsoniana 'Columnaris' 'Glauca'

High on any list of top ten conifers, this forms a narrow pillar of bluish grey foliage. It makes a fine specimen, but on the continent it is also used for screening and looks quite outstanding. Try it if you want **something a bit special**.

Chamaecyparis lawsoniana 'Ellwood's Gold'

A neat conical habit with foliage yellow in spring, yellowy green the rest of the year. Good for the rock and heather garden and an ideal tub specimen.

Chamaecyparis lawsoniana 'Ellwoodii'

Possibly one of the most popular conifers. The shape of the plant depends on where the cutting was taken, but it is mostly broadly conical and rich green with a bluish hue. Ideal tub specimen but not suitable for a small rockery.

Chamaecyparis lawsoniana 'Ellwoods Pillar'

A really dwarf 'Ellwoodii', much slower growing and narrow in habit with deep green foliage. Ideal for the rockery or conifer bed.

Chamaecyparis lawsoniana 'Erecta'

A deep green conifer with flame shaped habit. Makes a fine specimen or with other conifers.

Chamaecyparis lawsoniana 'Fletcheri'

This conifer makes a lovely specimen plant, forming a broad conical columnwith soft grey green foliage. Can be used in a tub.

Chamaecyparis lawsoniana 'Gnome'

Gnome the name, gnome the nature. A real dwarf with deep green, congested foliage, **ideal for the rock garden or even a sink garden**.

Chamaecyparis lawsoniana 'Golden Wonder'

A very beautiful Lawson with foliage bright gold, dulling slightly in winter. Makes a fine specimen plant or with other conifers and heathers.

Chamaecyparis lawsoniana 'Green Hedger'

An upright growing conifer with rich green foliage. A useful plant for hedging and screening.

Chamaecyparis lawsoniana 'Green Pillar'

A handsome conifer with flattened sprays of bright green foliage. It makes a good specimen tree and associates well with other conifers and heathers.

Chamaecyparis lawsoniana 'Lane'

Makes a fine specimen tree with feathery sprays of golden yellow foliage. Needs a sunny position for best colour.

Chamaecyparis lawsoniana 'Minima Aurea'

A real gem of a dwarf conifer, nearly as wide as it is tall, with tightly packed golden foliage. **A must** in the heather garden or rock garden.

Chamaecyparis lawsoniana 'Minima Glauca'

An excellent dwarf conifer, forming a dense, globular bush of sea green. Ideal for the conifer garden and rockery and can also be used in tubs.

Chamaecyparis lawsoniana 'New Golden Seedling'

This is a new variety. Quite fast growing with foliage golden green in winter, gold in summer, Makes a good screen or as a specimen.

Chamaecyparis lawsoniana 'Pembury Blue'

This blue lawson cypress has a fine conical shape with sprays of silvery blue foliage. Good specimen plant.

Chamaecyparis lawsoniana 'Pottenii'

A very decorative conifer with crowded sea green foliage in soft, feathery sprays. An outstanding specimen and useful tub plant.

Chamaecyparis lawsoniana 'Pygmaea Argentea'

This dwarf conifer is a real gem. The bluish green foliage is tipped silvery white, in our opinion the best dwarf variegated conifer. Useful for rock gardens, tubs or sink gardens.

Chamaecyparis lawsoniana 'Silver Threads'

A very attractive sport of Ellwood's Gold. Golden green foliage which is flecked creamy white. **Slow growing** with neat, compact, columnar habit.

Chamaecyparis lawsoniana 'Stardust'

A beautiful golden lawson forming a lovely column of gold. It holds its colour well in winter, and becomes brighter in summer.

Chamaecyparis lawsoniana 'Stewartii'

An elegant golden lawson which is bright gold in summer, yellow green in winter. Makes an excellent specimen tree.

Chamaecyparis lawsoniana 'Yellow Transparent'

This variety has a dense, soft yellowy green foliage in winter, much brighter in summer and makes a good tub specimen.

Chamaecyparis obtusa 'Nana Aurea'

The golden counterpart of C.o. nana gracilis and should not be confused with 'nana lutea' which is much smaller. This one forms a small tree of open habit with attractive fan-type foliage, bright gold at the tips when in full sun. This yellow bronzes with the first frosts to give an added beauty to the plant.

Chamaecyparis obtusa 'Nana Gracilis'

A very beautiful dwarf conifer with compact, deep rich green foliage in short, neat, shell like sprays.

Chamaecyparis obtusa 'Nana Lutea'

A beautiful slow growing conifer, with bright gold foliage that holds its colour well in winter. **A gem for the rock garden**.

Chamaecyparis pisifera 'Boulevard'

A very popular conifer with bright, steel blue foliage, soft to the touch, tingeing purple in winter. To keep at its best prune lightly each year.

Chamaecyparis pisifera 'Filifera Aurea'

A conifer with a difference. It has golden thread like foliage and spreads wider than it is high, to eventually become a real feature of your garden. May be prone to scorching in its early days.

Chamaecyparis pisifera 'Filifera Nana'

A very attractive conifer with green, thread like foliage. It forms a neat rounded, flat topped bush. Ideal for the heather and conifer garden.

Chamaecyparis pisifera 'Filifera Sungold'

A new variety forming a mop head of thread like foliage. Tends to lose its colour unless planted in full sun and some plants hold colour better than others.

Chamaecyparis pisifera 'Nana Aureovariegata'

A real gem forming a bun like shape with crowded sprays of gold tinged, green foliage. A must for the rockery and can be used in tubs or sink gardens.

Chamaecyparis pisifera 'Nana'

A real gem forming a dense green, bun like shape. A must for the rockery and can be used in tubs or sink gardens.

Chamaecyparis pisifera 'Plumosa Aurea Nana'

A compact, slow growing conifer with soft, feathery golden foliage, holding its colour in winter. At its best when pruned lightly each year.

Chamaecyparis pisifera 'Squarrosa Lombarts'

This conifer makes a broad bush of soft feathery foliage, blue grey in summer, turning purplish bronze in winter.

Chamaecyparis pisifera 'Squarrosa Sulphurea'

Broadly conical in shape, this cultivar is particularly beautiful in spring and summer when the young foliage turns from bluish green to bright sulphur. The feathery habit adds useful form to a large heather garden.

Chamaecyparis thyoides 'Andelyensis'

A slow growing conifer forming a narrow column of bluish green, turning slightly bronze in winter if in an open position.

Chimonanthus praecox

A very fragrant, deciduous shrub from China of compact, bushy habit, flowering at various times between November and March. The flowers are yellowish green, stained purple at the centre and are followed by the lustrous dark green leaves. Best with the protection of a sunny wall. The flowers are borne on the previous years growth and any **pruning should be carried out immediately after flowering.**

Choisya ternata

A very popular evergreen shrub, foliage dark green, aromatic when crushed. Sweetly scented, white flowers appear in May and often later in summer and autumn. Makes a good tub specimen.

Cistus 'Silver Pink'

A sun loving, evergreen with silver pink flowers in June and July. It thrives in a dry, sunny position once established.

Cistus 'Sunset'

This sun loving, evergreen shrub with magenta flowers in June and July is quite happy planted in a dry, sunny position.

Cistus laurifolius

A hardy evergreen shrub with white, saucer shaped flowers with yellow centres. Thrives in a sunny position and dryish soil.

Cistus purpureus

A sun loving plant which will tolerate dry conditions. Large rosy crimson flowers with a chocolate blotch appear in June and July.

Cistus x corbariensis

A useful sun loving plant ideal for a dry spot. The flowers are pure white with crimson tinted buds, opening from May to June. **One of the hardiest sun roses**.

Cistus x loretii

A sun loving plant with large white flowers with crimson blotches. Evergreen and ideal on sunny banks and quite happy on dry, poor soil once established. **Grows well on chalky soil**.

Colutea arborescens 'Copper Beauty'

A very easy to grow shrub with copper coloured, pea shaped flowers throughout the summer, followed by large, inflated seed pods. May be hard pruned in March to control growth.

Convolvulus cneorum

A very striking evergreen shrub with shiny silver leaves. Pinky white, funnel shaped flowers appear from May to Sept. This plant requires a sheltered site to do well and is also an attractive rock garden plant.

Cordyline australis

This evergreen with sword like leaves and white flowers in early summer, is used extensively on patios in tubs. **Needs a sheltered position in full sun** with good drainage, whether in a tub or open ground. The flower is not a main feature.

Cornus alba 'Elegantissima'

If you have a dull corner in your garden, this could be the right shrub. It grows in most conditions, has green, white mottled leaves, good autumn tints and red stems in winter. For really bright stems prune hard in spring.

Cornus alba 'Sibirica' ('Westonbirt')

A superb shrub for unusual winter colour. The stems of this plant are a brilliant red in winter, hidden by the leaves in summer. Best colour is held by the young stems.

Cornus alba 'Spaethii' (Gouchaltii)

A superb dogwood with red stems in winter and golden variegated foliage all summer. Good autumn colour too. **Will tolerate most conditions**.

Cornus canadensis

This is not strictly a shrub but a plant which renews itself annually from ground level to produce a carpet of fresh green leaves, studded by star like flowers in early summer, followed by clusters of vivid red fruits. The leaves become wine coloured in autumn. Succeeds well in shade and lime free soil.

Cornus controversa

A magnificent, tree like shrub, the sweeping branches are covered during May and June with broad clusters of cream coloured flowers, followed by black fruits. The foliage often turns rich red purple in autumn.

Cornus florida

This outstanding large shrub is not often planted, as it does take time to mature though well worth the wait. Each flower head has four conspicuous white, petal like bracts in May, followed by rich autumn tints.

Cornus florida 'Rainbow'

This exciting new shrub I first saw in Holland in 1982. It has large, variegated gold foliage, each flower has four conspicuous white, petal like bracts in May. Autumn colour has to be seen to be believed. Not freely available.

Cornus kousa

This is a real gem of a shrub, the numerous flowers, of which the white bracts are the most conspicuous part, are poised on slender, erect stalks, covering the spreading branches in June, followed by strawberry like fruits and rich, autumn colours.

Cornus kousa chinensis

A large elegant shrub with white bracts covering the spreading branches in June. Strawberry like fruits follow and the foliage turns rich colours in Autumn.

Cornus mas

A winter flowering cornus, yellow in colour on naked twigs in February, then bright red, cherry like fruits which are edible. The foliage turns red purple in autumn.

Cornus nuttallii

This plant can in time make a small tree. Large white bracts appear in May, sometimes flushed pink. The foliage turns yellow and occasionally red in autumn.

Cornus stonolifera 'Flaviramea'

A very attractive shrub with greeny yellow young stems which look particularly bright in winter, especially when planted with the red stemmed types of cornus. **Very good for a damp or wet spot, in sun or shade**.

Coronilla emerus

This free flowering shrub produces yellow pea like flowers throughout the growing season, followed by seed pods.

Cortaderia argentea (selloana)

A graceful, grass like plant with slender arching leaves, forming a dense mass of erect stems which carry the long silvery plumes.

Cortaderia selloana 'Gold Band'

A beautiful foliage plant from New Zealand. The leaves are edged bright golden yellow. The graceful silvery plumes are produced in late summer, rising above the foliage to about 5ft. This plant is tolerant of wet or dry soils,in sun or shade but probably best in full sun in a moist retentive soil.

Cortaderia selloana 'Rosea'

A tall, stately grass with tall flower spikes. This shows up best when grown with other cultivars. A less exciting plant than the name implies but well worth growing. **The plumes make excellent winter decoration when cut**. Can look magnificent if planted near water.

Corylopsis pauciflora

A very early spring flowering shrub, the yellow, cowslip scented flowers appearing in March before the small leaves. The young leaves are pink, turning green later.

Corylopsis willmottiae 'Spring Purple'

A very showy shrub for late winter colour. Soft yellow flowers in dense clusters, very sweetly scented, appear in March, April. The young growth of this form is an attractive plum purple.

Corylus avellana

A large shrub, very impressive when draped with its long catkins in February. Clusters of nuts follow, maturing in Sept. and Oct. Yellow autumn foliage.

Corylus avellana 'Contorta'

This is a real Jeykyll and Hyde plant. In winter a lovely shrub with its curiously twisted branches. In summer, however, it has rather ugly, large crinkled leaves.

Corylus maxima 'Purpurea'

A large shrub with large, deep purple leaves. Given time can be one of the most outstanding purple leaved shrubs.

Cotinus coggygria

A very colourful shrub with round, smooth leaves. Its fawn coloured, plume like flowers in June and July turn smokey grey in late summer. The foliage has excellent autumn tints.

Cotinus coggygria 'Notcutt's Variety'

An outstanding shrub with purple foliage. Unusual flowers appear in June and July, looking rather like puffs of smoke.

Cotinus coggygria 'Royal Purple'

An outstanding summer shrub with deep wine purple foliage, translucent in sunshine, the colour reddening in autumn. Purplish grey flowers appear in June and July, resembling puffs of smoke from a distance.

Cotoneaster 'Cornubia'

A semi evergreen shrub, vigorous in habit with white flowers in June followed by large red berries which can weigh down the branches. **Makes a good screening plant**.

Cotoneaster 'John Waterer'

A large semi evergreen shrub with long spreading branches. White flowers appear in June followed by bunches of red berries in autumn.

Cotoneaster 'Rothschildianus'

A large, evergreen shrub with white flowers in June, followed by creamy yellow berries. **Makes a good screen plant**.

Cotoneaster congestus

A very dwarf cotoneaster suitable for a rock garden. It has small, bright green, evergreen foliage on tightly packed branches which form a low, spreading mound. Small pink flowers appear in June, followed by red berries.

Cotoneaster congestus 'Nanus'

A delightful but difficult to find plant, in this form which makes a low growing dense mound with tiny bright green leaves, and slowly creeping sideways to cover rocks. The pale pink flowers appear in June and are much loved by bees. These are followed in the autumn by bright red fruits. A real gem for the rock garden.

Cotoneaster dammeri 'Coral Beauty'

An evergreen ground cover shrub with small leaves and somewhat arching branches. White flowers appear in spring, followed by orange red berries in autumn. **Ideal on steep banks** and other areas where it would be impossible to mow grass.

Cotoneaster franchetii

A very graceful semi evergreen with white flowers in June, followed by orange scarlet berries. Can be used for screening.

Cotoneaster horizontalis

A very popular planted shrub, very easy to please, low growing with masses of white flowers in spring, followed by red berries and rich autumn colour. Can be used as a wall plant or ground cover. **Excellent on north facing wall or fence**.

Cotoneaster horizontalis 'Variegatus'

An attractive variegated form of 'herringbone' with smaller, white edged leaves tinged pink. The foliage is particularly striking in autumn. Red berries adorn the plant for most of the winter. A useful plant for growing against a north facing wall or fence.

Cotoneaster lacteus

An excellent evergreen with large oval leathery leaves, grey tormentose beneath. White flowers are followed by large clusters of small red berries, lasting till after Christmas. Useful hedging and screening plant.

Cotoneaster salicifolius

A tall and graceful evergreen plant, variable in habit, with white flowers in June and red berries in autumn. Excellent screening plant.

Cotoneaster x watereri

A large shrub or small tree of vigorous growth, being semi-evergreen and bearing many orange/red or red fruits in the autumn following the white flowers in June.

Crataegus monogyna

The common Quickthorn or Hawthorn of our native hedgerows. Lovely in May when in flower and often laden with red fruit (haws) in the autumn. It is very prickly and well barbed.

Crinodendron hookeranum

This is a real gem of an evergreen, with flowers like long stalked crimson lanterns, hanging thickly along the branches in May. **Needs sheltered position and lime free soil**.

Cryptomeria japonica 'Elegans'

This attractive conifer has very soft feathery foliage, browny green in summer turning copper bronze in winter. **Makes a good lawn specimen**.

Cryptomeria japonica 'Globosa Nana'

This unusual conifer takes time to attain a definite form but makes a neat, rounded bush, wider than high. The branchlets are closely crowded and irregular, seeming to fall on top of each other.

Cryptomeria japonica 'Vilmoriniana'

A very fine dwarf conifer, making a tightly congested bush of rich green that turns red purple in winter. Ideal for the rock garden and sink garden.

Cupressocyparis leylandii

This is the fastest growing conifer in the country, used mainly for hedging and screening. **Withstands relatively poor sites**, and will take quite hard trimming.

Cupressocyparis leylandii 'Castlewellan'

This is an outstanding screening conifer with bright gold foliage in summer, yellow in winter. Also excellent specimen conifer. **Can be pruned to suit position**.

Cupressus macrocarpa 'Donard Gold'

An improvement on C. macrocarpa 'Lutea' and similar to 'Goldcrest' but slightly more open habit. It will form a conical or broadly columnar tree with deep golden yellow foliage if positioned in full sun. In shade the tree loses its spectacular colour.

Cupressus macrocarpa 'Goldcrest'

An outstanding, fast growing golden conifer with feathery juvenile foliage. **Makes a fine specimen in full sun**.

Cytisus 'Cornish Cream'

A small broom with cream coloured pea flowers, makes an outstanding display in May when in full flower.

Cytisus 'Daisy Hill'

A well known shrub with pink buds opening to cream, flushed pink, wings deep crimson, in May and June. Well drained soil and sunny position. **Best lightly pruned each year after flowering**.

Cytisus 'Dragonfly'

A strong growing broom with deep yellow flowers with crimson wings appearing in May and June. **Lightly prune after flowering to retain shape**.

Cytisus 'Fulgens', Standard

Forms a head with a mass of flowers reddish in bud, and opening orange/yellow. Flowering later than most brooms. Side shoots or suckers must be removed. Stake firmly and remember to prune.

Cytisus 'Golden Sunlight'

A strong growing upright broom with rich yellow flowers in spring. Ideal for a sunny dry site.

Cytisus 'Goldfinch'

A useful plant for a dry sunny spot. This broom has masses of yellow and red pea flowers in May.

Cytisus 'Goldfinch', Standard

Forms a head with masses of yellow and red flowers in May. Side shoots or suckers must be removed. Stake firmly and remember to prune.

Cytisus 'Hollandia'

A fine sun loving shrub with cream and cerise flowers in spring. **Very good for poor dry soil, in a sunny spot**.

Cytisus 'Killiney Red'

A fine broom with rich red flowers, the wings darker and velvety. Ideal for a sunny dry site.

Cytisus 'Minstead'

This charming broom produces masses of white, lilac flushed flowers in May and June. Best in full sun, well drained soil.

Cytisus 'Queen Mary'

An atractive hybrid broom with light yellow and brownish orange flowers. **Good for a dry sunny spot**.

Cytisus 'Redwings'

A hybrid broom with brilliant red flowers, quickly growing to 5 or 6ft. Requiring a position in full sun and good drainage. They are particularly useful for giving height to a newly planted shrub border but are liable to become untidy unless the new growths are pruned back immediately after flowering by about one half.

Cytisus 'Windlesham Ruby'

A showy hybrid broom with dark mahogany crimson, pea flowers in May and June.

Cytisus 'Zeelandia'

An attractive variety of the well known broom. The flowers are lilac outside, cream inside with pinkish wings and a cream keel.

Cytisus battandieri

A semi evergreen shrub, best grown with the protection of a south or west facing wall. The pea shaped flowers are bright yellow, borne in fat racemes and with the scent of pineapple. A further feature of this beautiful shrub are the large laburnum-like leaves which have three leaflets clothed with white silky hairs giving them a silvery appearance. Award of Garden Merit 1938.

Cytisus burkwoodii

Forms a mass of flowers of cerise with deep crimson wings.

Cytisus burkwoodii, Standard

Forms a head with a mass of flowers, cerise with deep crimson wings. Grafted onto Laburnum stock, any side shoots or suckers must be removed. Stake firmly and remember to prune.

Cytisus scoparius 'Andreanus'

A selective form of the common broom with attractive yellow and crimson flowers. This cultivar has been around for a long time and received a First Class Certificate from the R.H.S. in 1890.

Cytisus x kewensis

A semi prostrate broom producing sheets of cream coloured flowers in May. Suitable for a large rock garden or as ground cover.

Cytisus x praecox

This outstanding dwarf broom, forms in early May, a tumbling mass of rich cream flowers.

Cytisus x praecox 'Albus'

One of a group of hybrid brooms which first appeared in a Warminster nursery in 1867. In this instance the flowers are white. The plant forms a small shrub 3 to 4 ft. high and as much across, smothered with flowers in early May born on semi- pendulous branches.

Cytisus x praecox 'Allgold'

A small broom with arching sprays of long lasting yellow flowers in early summer. **Good for poor soil**.

Cytisus x praecox, Standard

Forms a loose head with masses of rich cream flowers in early May. Any side shoots or suckers must be removed. Stake firmly and **remember to prune**.

Daboecia species and cultivars

These plants are native of Ireland and are low growing with broad,fresh-green leaves and large urn-shaped flowers from June till frost. It **can suffer from cold in exposed positions**.

Daboecia cantabrica 'Atropurpurea'

A strong and bushy grower with dark, bronze green foliage. The flowers are a rich warm purple in strong spikes. A variety that can be relied upon to make a good show each summer.

Daphne cneorum

A very popular evergreen shrub of lax, prostrate habit. Rose-pink, highly scented flowers appear freely in May and June. The leaves are deep green and narrowly oblong in shape. **Ideal for chalky soils**.

Daphne mezereum

One of the best winter flowering shrubs, with purple red flowers in February and March. It is also very sweetly scented and quite happy growing on chalk.

Daphne odora 'Aureomarginata'

An evergreen shrub of lax habit. The flowers are fragrant, reddish purple on the outside fading to almost white within. The narrow, oval leaves are mid-green and have a thin cream-white margin. Although D. Odora is not completely hardy this variety is a hardier form.

Daphne odora 'Walberton'

A superb evergreen shrub, flowering in winter, early spring. The flowers are purple pink and very fragrant.

Daphne x burkwoodii

A medium sized semi evergreen shrub with very fragant pale pink flowers in clusters during May and June. Plenty of humus and moisture are required but the drainage must be good.

Deutzia 'Mont Rose'

This is a very easy to please shrub with rose pink flowers in June.

Deutzia gracilis 'Rosea'

A compact growing shrub with arching branches and pink, bell shaped flowers in early summer. **Very easy to please**.

Deutzia magnifica

A vigorous shrub of upright habit. It forms a fine spectacle in June when covered with large panicles of double white flowers.

Deutzia scabra 'Plena'

A tall, erect growing shrub with double white flowers, suffused rose purple outside. A very easy to please shrub.

Deutzia x kalmiiflora

A very beautiful free flowering shrub with quite large flowers pale rose within and deeper outside the petals. The flowers resemble Kalmia, whence the name of this hybrid raised by Lemoine in 1900. An extremely decorative June flowering plant and very hardy.

Diervilla x splendens

A hybrid between D.lonicera and D.sessilifolia. This forms a medium sized deciduous shrub with lemon-yellow flowers in clusters on the tips of the current seasons growth, which is bronze when young becoming green with maturity. Recommended for the middle or back of the border.

Elaeagnus ebbingei

A fast growing, evergreen shrub with dark green leaves, silver beneath. Flowers are small, silvery, scaly and possess a stephanotis like fragrance, appearing in autumn. Fruits are orange with silvery freckles in spring. **Excellent screening plant**.

Elaeagnus pungens 'Maculata'

A top ten shrub. Evergreen gold and green foliage, **superb winter colour**. Can be used for cutting for the house. Easy to grow.

Elaeagnus x ebbingei 'Limelight'

A fast growing evergreen shrub with dark green leaves which have a central blotch of yellow. Not so colourful as Elaeagnus Pungens Maculata but much more vigorous. A good screening plant. Small silvery flowers in autumn.

Embothrium coccineum 'Longifolium'

A spectacular evergreen shrub with bright scarlet flowers produced in masses during May and June. This type has longer leaves than the species and is also hardier, though it does nevertheless require a sheltered, sunny spot.

Enkianthus campanulatus

A splendid, upright growing shrub with cup shaped flowers, sulphur to rich bronze, carried in great profusion in May. **Useful for cutting**. **Excellent autumn colours**.

Erica arborea

Tall growing heathers from Spain and Portugal and therefore requiring some protection particularly when young. If planted in groups they provide mutual protection. They flower in spring.

Erica carnea cultivars

The winter flowering heather provide a colourful carpet of colour from January to April. They are very reliable and hardy and **will also accept some lime in the soil**.

Erica carnea

A chalk tolerant species with light pink flowers from November to May, giving valuable winter colour. The foliage may vary from light green, through bronze to dull yellow. This species is the parent of many fine cultivars and is found growing wild in many mountainous areas of Europe.

Erica carnea 'Ada Collins'

A compact growing heather with mid green foliage. The white flowers are numerous and well formed.

Erica carnea 'Ann Sparkes'

A slow growing, spreading heather, eventually making a fairly large plant, with yellow orange foliage turning to old gold with purple bronze leaf margins. The flowers are a rich purple but rather sparse.

Erica carnea 'Aurea'

A bushy, rather upright and spreading plant with light lime green or pale yellow foliage in summer, becoming yellow gold in winter with orange tints. The flowers are deep pink in short racemes.

Erica carnea 'December Red'

A vigorous plant with shining deep green foliage. The flowers - in strong spikes, are pink at first changing to bright rose red.

Erica carnea 'Foxhollow'

A low, vigorous and spreading plant with light yellow green foliage, which becomes rich yellow in winter. The flowers are white bells which on opening, slowly change to pale pink. A closer inspection of the flowers will show that there are two shades of pink.

Erica carnea 'Heathwood'

A lime tolerant heather with dark green foliage that turns bronze purple in winter. Strong spikes of bright rose purple flowers appear after Christmas, continuing till spring. **Makes attractive ground cover**.

Erica carnea 'James Backhouse'

A compact late winter flowering heather with pale green buds opening to rose coloured bell-shaped flowers. The foliage is a good mid-green.

Erica carnea 'King George'

An established heather that holds its own with the best. A compact plant with dark shining green foliage. The flowers are bell shaped, of deep rose pinkfreely produced on short spikes.

Erica carnea 'Loughrigg'

A moderately vigorous plant with mid green foliage, bronzed in winter. The flowers are rose purple bells in good spikes.

Erica carnea 'Myretoun Ruby'

Without doubt one of the finest introductions in recent years. The flowers have reddish brown buds which open to reveal the striking colour of the bells, rich pink, intensifying to a clear bright red. The foliage is very dark green.

Erica carnea 'Pink Spangles'

This heath has green buds developing into flowers which are bicoloured at first, the corolla pink and the calyx green. On maturity they become deep clear pink. The plant is vigorous and spreading with bright green foliage.

Erica carnea 'Praecox Rubra'

A compact, slow spreading plant with dark green foliage. The flowers although rather small are plentiful, dark reddish pink.

Erica carnea 'Prince of Wales'

Winter flowering with short spikes of shell pink flowers. The foliage is light green, often tipped with red. This is one of the slower growing heathers and will take time to build into a substantial plant.

Erica carnea 'Ruby Glow'

The name gives a clue to the colour of the flower. The flowers are as red as any ruby. A vigorous and spreading plant with dark green foliage.

Erica carnea 'Springwood Pink'

A popular plant that is **vigorous and spreading**. The flowers are white at first, changing to clear pink. The foliage is a mid green.

Erica carnea 'Springwood White'

The flowers are large, pure white, each corolla tipped with a bunch of pale brown anthers. They are borne on long spikes on dense trailing growth. The foliage is bright green.

Erica carnea 'Vivellii'

A superb plant. The flowers are deep carmine red on strong spikes. The shape is compact with pretty new growth. The foliage is dark green turning intensely bronze during winter.

Erica carnea 'Winter Beauty'

A very attractive winter flowering heather with closely packed sprays of bright rose flowers from early winter almost to spring. **Fairly slow spreading** ground cover.

Erica cinerea

A native plant growing throughout Britain. They begin to flower in June, so spring pruning must not be delayed. The spent flowers can be attractive in winter and **useful for** 'flower' decoration. Will accept drier conditions than most heathers.

Erica cinerea 'Alba Minor'

The white flowers in clusters, are often so massed as to obscure the foliage. The form is small but extremely compact, with light apple green foliage.

Erica cinerea 'Atrosanguinea'

Sometimes known as 'Atrosanguinea Smith's Variety', this plant has a low, open habit with dark green foliage. The flowers are bright red, the flowering shoots arch and, when the first flush of bells begin to fade, new stems appear with yet another crop.

Erica cinerea 'C.D. Eason'

One of the most popular of the brighter colour bell heathers. A free growing plant with deep green foliage and masses of brilliant, deep pink flowers.

Erica cinerea 'Contrast'

A plant with dark green foliage and a profusion of bell shaped flowers, a rich dark shade of purple.

Erica cinerea 'Hookstone White'

The white flowers are bell shaped and pure white. Although individually small they are produced in quantity on a long raceme. The foliage is pale green, darkening with maturity.

Erica cinerea 'Pink Foam'

An open, loose growing plant with dark green foliage. The flowers are pale pink, almost white, tinged with rose at the base.

Erica cinerea 'Pink Ice'

A neat, compact and generous flowering plant with flowers deep, clear pink on opening, becoming paler - the colour of pink coconut ice. The foliage is mid green with silver reverse.

Erica cinerea 'Stephen Davis'

This heather can hardly be surpassed for its sheer brilliance of colour. The flowers are compact, bright red with purple or maroon shades and the foliage is deep, glossy green.

Erica cinerea 'Velvet Night'

The flowers of this plant have one of the darkest colours to be found amongst all heaths - a dark maroon purple. The foliage is dark glossy green, formed in a neat bushy habit.

Erica erigena (mediterranea)

These plants occur in the wild from western Ireland through northern Spain into south-west France. It **grows well on soils containing lime** and makes excellent ground cover flowering from April to June.

Erica erigena (mediterranea) 'Brightness'

A plant whose habit is neat, upright and elliptical in shape, with grey green foliage becoming purple in winter. The flowers are bright purple pink, opening from dark brown buds.

Erica erigena (mediterranea) 'Golden Lady'

An attractive heather with bright yellow foliage that darkens in a sunny location. The small white flowers are borne on long spikes.

Erica erigena (mediterranea) 'Irish Dusk'

A tall growing plant that is particularly **suitable for a dwarf hedge**, with pink flowers borne on long stems. The foliage is a dark green.

Erica erigena (mediterranea) 'W.T.Rackliff'

The flowers are large white bells with characteristic protruding brown anthers, borne in short crowded spikes. They are so profuse as to cover the bush each spring. The growth is neat and rounded with rich green foliage.

Erica lusitanica

An elegant large growing heather with light fresh green foliage. The flowers are deep red in bud opening pure white and slightly fragrant. **Upright habit** with the ends of the branches often stained red during the winter.

Erica tetralix 'Alba Mollis'

A tight, compact and rather upright heather that is quite indipensible in the heather garden. The foliage is light silver becoming greener with age.

Erica tetralix 'Con Underwood'

A superb, free flowering form that can be recommended for a **long lasting display**. The plant has a neat, upright habit with grey green foliage. The flowers are crimson purple bells.

Erica vagans

Natives of Cornwall and also parts of France and Spain, these are spreading plants flowering from August to October. They will tolerate a very small amount of lime in the soil but are better under acid conditions.

Erica vagans 'Lyonesse'

A tall, upright and **fairly quick growing** heather, the white flowers have gold anthers. The flowers must be a good source of honey, judging by the number of bees they attract.

Erica vagans 'Mrs D.F. Maxwell'

This outstanding plant with deep glossy green foliage and cerise - dark red flowers, has neat bushy growth with long spikes. Possibly the most popular summer flowering variety.

Erica vagans 'St. Keverne'

A compact, bushy plant with fresh, vivid green foliage and an abundance of bright rose flowers. Many pink cultivars have been raised, but few come anywhere near this in quality of flower and general appearance.

Erica vagans 'Valerie Proudley'

The growth is fairly slow, eventually making a small dense bush with white flowers. The foliage is of a particularly bright nature - especiallly in winter. The new growth is light gold and the older foliage lime green.

Erica x darleyensis

The 'winter flowering hybrid' heathers are mostly taller growing than Erica Carnea, neat and tidy in growth and tolerant of a range of garden conditions and soils. They make excellent ground cover.

Erica x darleynsis 'Arthur Johnson'

A justly popular heather. The flowers are bright mauve pink in very long spikes, and may be cut for the house as well as garden decoration. The foliage is a light green.

Erica x darleynsis 'Darley Dale'

Vigorous, bushy and ideal for ground cover in the most difficult locations. The flowers are pale rose purple, becoming deeper towards the end of the season. The foliage is a deep green.

Erica x darleynsis 'Furzey'

One of the richest colours to be found in this group. The flowers are dark rose purple bells in strong spikes. The foliage is dark green, turning even darker in the winter.

Erica x darleynsis 'George Rendall'

The foliage is fresh green, tipped red in winter, with the new growth in spring tipped yellow and pink. The flowers are lilac pink in dense profusion on tapering spikes. **Long flowering and reliable** no matter what the weather.

Erica x darleynsis 'Ghost Hills'

The short spikes are crowded with deep rose bells, becoming red at times. The first flowers open during the late autumn, then after a short lull provide a generous display in spring. The foliage is bright green.

Erica x darleynsis 'Jack H. Brummage'

The summer colouring of the foliage is light yellow, turning golden green or clear gold in the winter. In cold weather red tints can be seen. The flowers are deep pink in short spikes.

Erica x darleynsis 'Silberschmelze'

Known also as 'Silver - Bells / Beads / Mist / Star', this is a neatly rounded plant with silver white flowers with brown anthers, carried on good strong spikes. The foliage is deep, glossy green.

Erica x watsonii

Natural hybrids originally discovered by H.C. Watson near Truro, Cornwall in 1832 are valuable summer flowering heathers.

Erica x watsonii 'Dawn'

The flowers are deep rose pink, in large rounded bells. New growth foliage is clear yellow with tangerine tips becoming a deeper green with age. A plant with a **compact bushy habit**.

Escallonia 'Apple Blossom'

A very attractive and useful evergreen with glossy green foliage. Pink and white flowers appear in summer and autumn. Makes a good hedging plant.

Escallonia 'C.F.Ball'

A seedling of E. macrantha with crimson flowers. A vigorous growing cultivar. The large leaves are aromatic when bruised. Received Award of Merit in 1926.

Escallonia 'Crimson Spire'

A strong growing evergreen shrub with dark, glistening green foliage. Bright crimson flowers appear over a long period. Ideal for hedging.

Escallonia 'Donard Radiance'

A superb strong growing evergreen shrub with chalice-shaped flowers of brilliant rich pink. Similar in habit to E. Apple Blossom with which it would make an attractive evergreen hedge in a sheltered position, Award of Merit 1954.

Escallonia 'Donard Seedling'

A very fine evergreen shrub with glossy green foliage. **Ideal for brightening up a shrub border** as it flowers over a long period. The flowers are pink in bud, opening white. Can also be used for hedging.

Escallonia 'Donard Star'

A lovely evergreen shrub growing to 5 or 6 feet, with deep rosy-pink flowers about 1 ins across. Having a compact habit of growth, this cultivar will make a excellent 5 ft. hedge in a sheltered position. In bad winters much of the foliage will fall. One of several E. x langleyensis hybrids bred by the Slieve Donard Nursery, Ireland.

Escallonia 'Iveyi'

A vigorous, evergreen shrub with white flowers in late summer and autumn and large, glossy leaves.

Escallonia 'Langleyensis'

A long flowering evergreen with pink flowers from June to September. Can be used for screening.

Escallonia 'Pride of Donard'

A gem of an evergreen with large green, polished leaves. The flowers are large for Escallonias, brilliant rose coloured, very long flowering period. A good hedging plant.

Escallonia 'Red Elf'

A fine, red flowered evergreen forming a compact shrub. Can be used to make a colourful hedge.

Escallonia macrantha

A fast growing evergreen shrub with large, glossy green leaves. The rose crimson flowers are produced over a long period. The foliage is slightly aromatic when crushed. Can also be used for hedging.

Escallonia rubra 'Woodside

This is one of the smallest of the Escallonias. It has a compact habit, is evergreen and produces masses of small crimson flowers in summer. Can be used on a large rock garden.

Eucalypyus gunnii

This hardy gum can be grown as a tree or shrub, as a shrub it's ever blue foliage is quite startling all year. **Can be used for flower arranging**.

Eucryphia x nymansensis 'Nymansay'

An outstanding large shrub, evergreen with white flowers and yellow stamens in August and September. Needs sheltered position.

Euonymus alatus (alata)

A superb, slow growing shrub, producing perhaps the most brilliant autumn colour display of any plant. The stems are angular with broken ridges of corky bark that run along the length of every branch. Purple fruits with scarlet seeds follow the insignificant flowers.

Euonymus europaeus 'Red Cascade'

A selected form of the native Spindle tree raised by Jackmans of Woking, which is very free-fruiting. It makes a vigorous green stemmed shrub or small tree with branches which can become pendulous with the weight of the fruit which is bright red and orange in autumn, when the leaves also colour well. Award of Garden Merit 1969.

Euonymus fortunei 'Emerald Gaiety'

A dwarf, evergreen shrub with green and silvery white foliage, **excellent as ground cover** or with dwarf conifers or heathers.

Euonymus fortunei 'Emerald and Gold'

A dwarf shrub with gold and green foliage. Excellent as ground cover or with dwarf conifers or heathers.

Euonymus fortunei 'Silver Queen'

A very fine, variegated shrub with bright creamy yellow new growth, becoming green with broad creamy margins. Sometimes pale green flowers appear, followed by pinkish capsules with orange seeds. Makes a fine wall plant.

Euonymus fortunei 'Sun Spot'

Similar in habit to Emerald Gaiety and Emerald and Gold but slightly taller. The dark olive-green leaves have a bold central splash of golden yellow, which create a sparkling evergreen effect throughout the seasons. Grows easily and well in sun or part shade. An occasional trim is beneficial, once established.

Euonymus fortunei 'Variegatus'

A dwarf evergreen with green and creamy white marked foliage. Excellent in front of larger shrubs and goes well with conifers and heathers. If grown against a wall or stump it will climb.

Euonymus japonica 'Albomarginatus'

An evergreen shrub of densely leafy habit. A handsome bush for a sheltered spot with dark polished green leaves with a thin margin of white. The flowers are greenish white, followed by pinkish berries , but these are insignificant compared with the foliage. Introduced from Japan in 1804, it is an excellent sea side shrub and is only occasionally damaged by frost in the south of England.

Euonymus japonica 'Microphyllus Variegatus'

An attractive evergreen shrub with very small, white edged leaves. It grows in very much the same way as box. Ideal in containers and with other dwarf shrubs.

Euonymus japonica 'Ovatus Aureus'

A slow growing evergreen with yellow and green leaves, upright in growth, needs a sunny spot to keep its colour.

Euonymus japonicus 'Aureopictus'

A beautiful evergreen shrub that makes a good tub specimen. The glossy green leaves have a yellow centre and provide valuable winter colour.

Fagus sylvatica

An outstanding hedging plant, bright green all summer. Outstanding autumn colour, holding the leaves till the following spring.

Fagus sylvatica 'Purpurea'

A slow growing hedging plant with copper purple leaves all summer holding the old foliage till the following spring.

Fatsia japonica 'Variegata'

A variegated form of Fatsia with large shiny leaves edged with cream. **A useful plant for a sheltered shady spot**. Can also be grown in a tub.

Fatsia japonica (Aralia sieboldii)

A handsome evergreen shrub with large, shining green leaves. Heads of ball like white flowers appear in September or October on mature plants. Needs a sheltered spot **but does well in sun or shade**. Can be grown in a tub and is often grown as a cool houseplant.

Forsythia 'Lynwood'

This variety of the well known forsythia has large, rich yellow flowers in March. A very easy to please shrub.

Forsythia x intermedia 'Spectabilis'

When we see the forsythias in flower, we know winter is behind us. Masses of large, bright yellow flowers in March. **Very easy to please**.

Fothergilla major

A rather unusual shrub with its white, bottle brush like flowers, which appear before the leaves in spring. It also **has outstanding autumn tints**.

Fremontodendron 'California Glory'

An evergreen or semi evergreen climbing shrub with rich yellow mallow like flowers. It **requires a warm South or South-west facing wall** and well drained soil. The hairs on the young leaves give a silvery appearance.

Fuchsia 'Alice Hoffman'

One of the most colourful shrubs, with semi double, scarlet and white, bell shaped flowers and purple tinged foliage. Free flowring from late June to October. Cover roots with dry peat or bracken from November till spring for protection.

Fuchsia 'Brilliant'

A vigorous hardy variety with scarlet sepals and violet magenta skirt with red veining. **Very good for a shady spot**.

Fuchsia 'Chillerton Beauty'

A very attractive hardy fuchsia, the flowers are single with pale pink sepals, the corolla opens purple and matures to magenta. A well known variety first introduced in 1847.

Fuchsia 'Constance'

This double fuchsia was introduced from the U.S.A. in 1935. A sport of Pink Pearl, the corolla is rosy-mauve with pink tints at the base, the sepals pale pink with green tips. Free flowering, the growth is bushy and upright and **easy to grow**.

Fuchsia 'Corallina'

A fuchsia with a spreading habit, so it can be grown as colourful ground cover or be staked to grow more upright. The flower is single, carmine red and purple. The foliage is very dark green.

Fuchsia 'Drame'

A vigorous and free flowering hardy fuchsia with scarlet sepals and purplish red corolla or skirt. The foliage is yellowish green when new and medium green as it matures. The plant is bushy and self branching.

Fuchsia 'Genii'

A hardy Fuchsia with golden foliage and single flowers with cerise sepals and a purple corolla or skirt. The plant makes a sturdy, self branching bush. The leaf colour is **best in the open garden and in full sun**.

Fuchsia 'Lady Thumb'

A very attractive 'sport' of the fuchsia 'Tom Thumb'. The flower is semi-double, carmine pink with a white, pink veined corolla. The plant is small and compact enough to be planted in a rock garden and produces flowers through the summer and well into autumn.

Fuchsia 'Lena'

A semi double hardy fuchsia with pale flesh pink sepals and rosy magenta flushed pink corolla or skirt. The growth is lax and it can be used for hanging baskets. Very free flowering and **a must for every collection**.

Fuchsia 'Madame Cornelissen'

A hardy, large flowered fuchsia with red and white bell flowers from late June to October. Cover roots with dry peat or bracken from November till spring for protection.

Fuchsia 'Margaret Brown'

A self branching, bushy, upright and very free flowering variety. The flower is single, small and two shades of pink. A delightfu plant for the **sheltered shrub border**.

Fuchsia 'Margaret'

A large flowered hardy fuchsia with a rose coloured calyx and double mauve corolla or skirt, **flowering from June to Octber**. In winter cover the roots with dry peat or bracken for protection.

Fuchsia 'Mrs Popple'

A very popular variety with large violet purple and crimson flowers from late June to October. Cover roots with dry peat or bracken from November till spring for protection.

Fuchsia 'Peter Pan'

A basket fuchsia which is vigorous and free flowering with bright green foliage. The single flowers are medium sized with long broad upturned pink sepals and a corolla of orchid and lilac mauve. Introduced in 1960 by Ericson.

Fuchsia 'Pixie'

A hardy fuchsia with single flowers introduced in 1960. A sport of Graf White,the corolla is rosy mauve paler at the base and the tube and sepals pale cerise. Medium sized flowers and free flowering. The growth is vigorousupright and bushy. This variety would make an attractive 3ft. hedge.

Fuchsia 'Prosperity'

A double flowered hardy fuchsia. The sepals are crimson and the skirt is pale pink, veined with rose red. An upright and free flowering hybrid which **will do best in a sheltered spot**. Cover the roots with dry peat, bracken or leaves during the winter for extra protection.

Fuchsia 'Riccartonii'

This is classed as the hardiest of fuchsias and in the west country is used as hedging. It very often gets cut down to ground level in winter. Masses of small, red and purple bell flowers appear from June to October.

Fuchsia 'Tennessee Waltz'

A hardy Fuchsia which should be in every collection. The semi-double to double, medium sized flowers are rose red with a lilac lavender corolla splashed rose. A strong upright grower and easy to train. Once in flower it will continue through the season. Highly commended in the hardy fuchsia trials by the R.H.S. in 1965.

Fuchsia 'Tom Thumb'

This fuchsia is **a real gem**, dwarf habit, masses of red and purple, bell shaped flowers from June to October. Cover roots with dry peat or bracken from November till spring for protection.

Fuchsia magellanica

A **very hardy** and vigorous variety. In the south west of England it will often be grown as a hedge. In cooler areas it will be cut down to ground level by frost, shooting up again in the spring. The flowers are single, scarlet and violet.

Fuchsia magellanica 'Gracilis'

A natural variant of F. magellanica having slightly longer flowers and deeper purple corolla or skirt but similar deep red sepals. It is also a little more slender in growth than the type. **One of the hardiest Fuchsias**.

Fuchsia magellanica 'Variegata'

A very striking, variegated shrub, leaves green, margined creamy yellow, flushed pink. The flowers are small, scarlet and purple, produced from late June to October. Cover roots with dry peat or bracken from November till spring for protection.

Fuchsia magellanica 'Versicolor' (tricolor)

A very interesting hardy fuchsia with grey leaves, heavily stained red and pink, turning green and cream on maturity. Single, red and purple flowers appear in summer. An attractive feature even when not in flower.

Garrya elliptica

An outstanding evergreen, male plants produce long, grey green catkins in January and February. **Excellent for covering a north facing wall** or fence.

Garrya elliptica 'James Roof'

This variety of Garrya produces extra long catkins in January and February, as well as having large, evergreen, leathery leaves. It makes a good wall or fence plant, especially north facing.

Gaultheria procumbens

High on any top ten list, excellent ground cover, green foliage tinged crimson in winter. White flowers in late spring, early summer, followed by red berries all winter. Needs a moist position and lime free soil.

Gaultheria shallon

A vigorous evergreen shrub with broad leathery leaves. It is a valuable ground cover plant forming a dense thicket. Pale pink or white flowers hang in clusters during May or June, followed by purplish black berries.

Genista aetnesis

A large, elegant shrub with yellow, pea flowers in June. Needs a sunny, dry position to be at its best.

Genista hispanica

An excellent plant for a dry, sunny bank where it will produce abundant yellow flowers every May and June. It forms a very prickly, dense mound about 2 feet high, and earned an Award of Garden Merit in 1969.

Genista lydia

An outstanding dwarf shrub, semi prostrate and smothered in golden yellow flowers in May and June. Needs a sunny position and **will grow well on poor, dry soil** once established.

Genista pilosa

There seems to be more than one form of this shrub. This one is very prostrate, growing only a few inches high with golden yellow flowers in June. **Excellent ground cover** on dry, sunny banks or rockeries.

Genista tinctoria 'Plena'

A superb, semi prostrate shrub with double, yellow flowers from June to September. Excellent ground cover on dry, sunny banks or rockeries.

Genista tinctoria 'Royal Gold'

A small shrub producing masses of rich yellow pea flowers in summer. **Ideal for a dry sunny spot**.

Ginkgo biloba

This tree does not resemble in any way the average picture of a conifer, but is the oldest of all, going back 150 million years. It is deciduous, with fan shaped leaves of pale green, turning a beautiful butter yellow in autumn.

Griselinia littoralis

A lovely evergreen with an upright habit and apple green foliage. Not grown for its flower which is inconspicuous, but for the foliage which is excellent.

Griselinia littoralis 'Variegata'

A very beautiful evergreen foliage shrub. The leaves are apple green with conspicuous white varigation. The flowers are insignificant. The plant comes from New Zealand and **requires a sheltered position**.

Hamamelis mollis

A handsome, winter flowering shrub with sweetly scented, yellow flowers from December to March. Foliage turns rich yellow in autumn.

Hamamelis mollis 'Pallida'

An outstanding witch hazel with very fragrant, sulphur yellow flowers from December to March. **Can be cut for the house.**

Hamamelis x intermedia 'Diane'

A strong growing shrub with spidery, copper red flowers, produced from December to March on bare twigs. The foliage colours richly in autumn.

Hebe 'Autumn Glory'

A small, evergreen shrub with intense violet blue flowers in late summer and autumn. **Best when hard pruned in spring**.

Hebe 'Carl Teschner'

A very attractive hebe, which makes good ground cover. It has a low, spreading habit and produces masses of violet blue flowers, each with a white throat, on short spikes during June and July.

Hebe 'Gauntletii'

An attractive evergreen shrub requiring a sheltered position. Pink spikes of flowers are borne from June to October.

Hebe 'Great Orme'

A compact, upright form of hebe that is hardy and tolerates salty sea winds. Bright pink flowers in long spikes appear from late May or early June to October.

Hebe 'Marjorie'

A hardy evergreen Hebe which forms a rounded bush. Light violet and white flowers appear from July to Sept.

Hebe 'Midsummer Beauty'

Long racemes of lavender flowers lasting thoughout the summer. Light green leaves, reddish beneath. Received Award of Merit in 1960.

Hebe 'Mrs. Winder'

An attractive hybrid grown for its winter foliage colours more than its flower. The leaves and stems turn a rich purple during autumn, staying so till spring. The flowers are bright blue in small clusters during summer.

Hebe 'Purple Queen'

A very lovely evergreen shrub with glossy, green and purple foliage. Very showy, deep purple flowers appear in summer.

Hebe 'Simon Delaux'

A small shrub with rich crimson flowers in large clusters from July to September. The habit is compact and rounded.

Hebe 'White Gem'

Possibly a hybrid between H. brachysiphon and H. pinguifolia, this makes a neat ground cover if massed. Individually it forms a compact shrub about 18 inches high and bears white flowers in profusion in June.

Hebe albicans

A very good dwarf shrub with glaucous foliage and a rounded habit. White flowers appear in June and July. A good rockery plant.

Hebe franciscana 'Blue Gem'

A small evergreen which is **one of the hardiest Hebes**. Bright blue flowers appear from June to October.

Hebe franciscana 'Variegata'

A small evergreen with green, creamy white edged leaves. Pale blue flowers appear in late summer. Ideal for planting in tubs or troughs in a sheltered position.

Hebe ochracea 'James Stirling'

A superb evergreen shrub for summer and winter colour. The foliage is 'whipcord' like, bright green in summer, turning bronze ochre in winter.

Hebe pinquifolia 'Pagei'

A very hardy Hebe with blue grey, evergreen foliage and small, white flowers in May. Excellent ground cover for a rockery or when planted with shrubs.

Hebe rakaiensis (subalpina)

A small, dwarf, dense growing evergreen with pale green leaves. White flowers in dense clusters appear in June and July.

Hebe salicifolia

A hardy evergreen shrub with light green, willow like leaves. White, lilac tinged flowers appear from June to August.

Hebe veitchii

A small evergreen shrub producing spikes of bright blue flowers from July to October. **Ideal for brightening up the shrub border** in late summer when many plants are past their best.

Hebe x andersonii 'Variegata'

A strong growing shrub if given some protection but **susceptible to cold winds**. The leaves are broadly margined and splashed creamy-white. The long racemes of lavender blue flowers are produced in August and September. Much used as a bedding plant when young.

Hedera canariensis 'Variegata'

A strikingly attractive evergreen ground cover plant. The fairly large leaves are marked with green, grey and creamy white.

Hedera colchica 'Dentata Variegata'

A large leaved ivy looking similar to H. canariensis 'Variegata' but much hardier. The leaves are bright green shading to grey, edged creamy yellow when young, maturing creamy white.

Hedera colchica 'Paddy's Pride' (Sulphur Heart)

A large leaved form with variegated leaves, each with an irregular central splash of yellow. Can be used as ground cover or as a climber where it will cover walls, trees etc.

Hedera helix 'Anna Marie'

An evergreen climber that also makes an excellent ground cover plant. The small leaves are edged creamy white. It is **useful for dry shady spots**.

Hedera helix 'Arborescens'

A non climbing form of the common ivy. It has glossy, deep green, evergreen foliage, setting off the spiky, ball like heads of flowers. This plant makes excellent ground cover, forming a low, spreading mound, **very good under trees** and on dry banks.

Hedera helix 'Boskoop'

An attractive, small leaved form of ivy with green, pale veined leaves, many of them crimped, folded and waved. Ivies are very good evergreen ground cover plants, especially for shady areas, though they also climb well.

Hedera helix 'Cavendishii'

A very pretty ivy with leaves variegated green, grey and yellow in a sort of mottled pattern. It is a good ground cover plant, giving year round colour with its evergreen leaves, but will also climb and can be put in tubs, troughs and hanging baskets.

Hedera helix 'Cristata'

An unusual form of ivy with pale green, rather rounded leaves, waved and frilled at the edges. It can be used as ground cover even under trees and is also a good climber.

Hedera helix 'Deltoidea'

A distinctive looking ivy with rounded, almost heart shaped green leaves, which remain all winter. Makes excellent ground cover in areas where grass is impossible, ie on banks, under trees etc.

Hedera helix 'Gavotte'

A fairly small leaved ivy with smooth, shiny green, heart shaped leaves. A good plant for growing either as ground cover or as a climbing plant. Can also be used in tubs or troughs.

Hedera helix 'Glacier'

An evergreen climber that is also a good ground cover plant. The small leaves are green, grey and white. **Very versatile**, can be used in tubs and troughs, to cover walls and fences and even as a houseplant and hanging basket plant.

Hedera helix 'Goldheart'

A striking evergreen plant which may be used as ground cover even under trees. It is also good for hanging baskets, tubs, troughs and for climbing up walls, fences etc. Each green leaf has a central splash of yellow, often tingeing pink in winter.

Hedera helix 'Green Ripple'

An evergreen plant that may be used as ground cover in sun or shade. The ripply green leaves have prominent veins giving a good effect when massed. Ivies are very good evergreen ground cover plants, especially for a shady, dry site, ie under a tree, as well as climbing up walls, trees etc. and planting in tubs.

Hedera helix 'Ivalace'

An unusual looking ivy with small, delicate leaves with rolled in edges. The foliage is deep green and shiny, lasting all year. Makes a very attractive ground cover plant but will also climb if required.

Hedera helix 'Little Picture'

A small leaved form of ivy with leaves giving an overall frilly effect. A good evergreen ground cover plant which is also a climber. May be used to good effect in tubs and troughs.

Hedera helix 'Lutzii'

A useful evergreen ground cover plant that is also a good climber. The leaves are mottled grey green with splashes of yellow and green. Good for sun or shade especially under trees. May be planted in tubs and troughs for year round colour.

Hedera helix 'Sagittifolia'

A very pretty ivy with five lobed leaves, the centre lobe being long and triangular. The foliage is evergreen and the plant makes good ground cover, though it will also climb if given support.

Hibiscus syriacus 'Blue Bird'

An outstanding, sun loving shrub with single, violet blue flowers with a darker eye. Needs full sun and will flower from July to October.

Hibiscus syriacus 'Coelestis'

A superb, sun loving shrub. Violet blue, single flowers with a reddish base appear from July to October. Plant in well drained soil in full sun.

Hibiscus syriacus 'Hamabo'

An excellent, single flowered hybrid with large, pale pink flowers featuring a crimson blotch on each petal. Flowering occurs from July to October making a fine display.

Hibiscus syriacus 'Monstrosus'

A late summer flowering shrub with large, single white flowers with a maroon eye, apearing from July to October. **Requires full sun to give its best**.

Hibiscus syriacus 'Red Heart'

A lovely, sun loving plant with white, red centred flowers and an upright habit. Superb in late summer and autumn when many shrubs are past their best.

Hibiscus syriacus 'Woodbridge'

A lovely deciduous shrub with rich rose pink flowers, deepening in colour at the centre. **The flowers make a superb display in late summer and early autumn**.

Hydrangea 'Blue Wave'

A strong growing shrub producing beautifully shaped heads of blue fertile flowers, which give the effect of a lace cap. On acid soil the colour is gentian blue.

Hydrangea aspera

A superb hydrangea that can be rather variable in form. The large heads of pale blue flowers have an outer ring of lilac pink or white ray florets and appear from June to July. The leaves are large and felty with a light grey underside.

Hydrangea hortensis (mixed)

The well known mophead hydrangea comes in a range of colours. The colour stated on the label is the colour of the flower when the plant is in a neutral pH soil. On alkaline soils the blue types will tend to go either completely pink or just purplish. To these, blueing powder should be added as per the directions on the pack. The flowers are **good for dried flower arrangements**.

Hydrangea hortensis 'Alpengluchen'

A fine hydrangea with red flowers appearing from July to September. **A useful tub specimen**.

Hydrangea hortensis 'Altona'

A fine variety of the mop headed Hydrangea. The large flowers are normally pink, but this **is a good variety to treat with blueing powder**.

Hydrangea hortensis 'Blue Prince'

The colour of this variety will vary from cornflower blue on acid soils to rose red on chalk. The flowers appear from July to September.

Hydrangea hortensis 'Chaperon Rouge'

A very attractive red flowered form of the mop headed hydrangea, the flowers appearing in summer and early autumn. Can be grown in a tub.

Hydrangea hortensis 'Europa'

A superb hydrangea with deep pink heads of flowers appearing in summer and early autumn. **The colour may vary to pale blue on acid soils**.

Hydrangea hortensis 'Gen. Vicomtesse de Vibraye'

A mop head Hydrangea with vivid rose flowers which become a good blue when treated or in acid soil. This culivar received an Award of Merit from the R.H.S. in 1947. **Very free flowering**.

Hydrangea hortensis 'Gertude Glahn'

One of our most popular shrubs with large, mop headed flowers from pink to purple, varying a great deal with the acidity of the soil.

Hydrangea hortensis 'Hamburg'

A very large flowered hydrangea with deep rose to purple, mop headed flowers. To keep its purple blue colour, use a blueing powder every seven to fourteen days during the growing season.

Hydrangea hortensis 'Heinrich Seidel'

A mop head Hydrangea with heads of glowing red to purple flowers. The florets are large and fringed. **This cultivar does best in semi shade**.

Hydrangea hortensis 'King George'

Another one of our most popular shrubs with large, rose pink, mop head flowers from July to September. **Can be used as dried, cut flowers for the house**.

Hydrangea hortensis 'Madame Emile Moulliere'

A deservedly popular hydrangea. The large florets heve serrated sepals, white with a pink or blue eye. A good tub specimen.

Hydrangea paniculata 'Grandiflora'

One of the showiest hardy shrubs, massive panicles of sterile florets appear in summer and autumn, white, fading to pink. For best results, the laterals should be cut back to within 3'-4' of the previous season's growth. **Good for cutting for the house**.

Hydrangea serrata 'Bluebird'

A small robust shrub with quite outstanding lacecap flowers. The flower colour is blue on acid soils, reddish purple on chalk.

Hydrangea serrata 'Preziosa'

This is a very attractive hybrid with purplish red stems and young leaves purple tinged. Rounded heads of large, rose pink florets appear in summer, turning reddish purple in autumn.

Hydrangea villosa

One of the loveliest of late summer flowering shrubs, with large, lilac blue heads of flowers with prettily toothed marginal sepals. **Best grown in semi shade**.

Hypericum 'Hidcote'

A superb, semi evergreen shrub with large, golden yellow flowers from July to October. **Very easy to please**.

Hypericum beanii 'Gold Cup'

A very graceful small shrub, which produces its yellow cup like flowers over a long period.

Hypericum calycinum

This evergreen, dwarf shrub **will grow in almost any conditions**: sunny dry banks, heavily shaded positions, and will spread over wide areas with its bright yellow flowers in summer and autumn.

Hypericum inodorum 'Elstead'

A superb hypericum with pale yellow flowers in clusters from July to October. Brilliant salmon red fruits appear from late July.

Hypericum moseranum 'Tricolor'

A very colourful shrub with white, pink and green foliage. Yellow flowers appear from June to October, but this plant is grown more for the foliage than the flower.

Hypericum prolificum

A medium growing semi-evergreen bush, 3 to 5 feet high from the East and central United States with bright yellow flowers, about 1 inch across. The long leaves are dark shining green. A healthy and vigorous shrubs which bears enormous quantities of fruit. As the plants mature it features attractive grey pealing bark on the stems. Introduced about 1750.

Ilex aquifolium

The common holly can make a small tree or be kept to shrub size. An excellent, evergreen hedging plant. May produce berries in autumn.

Ilex aquifolium 'Argenteomarginata'

This broad leaved silver holly is a fine foliage plant. The female plant produces red berries but not to be relied on. **Can be planted as a hedge or grown as a tree**.

Ilex aquifolium 'Green Pillar'

A erect growing female form with dark green spiny leaves. The branches are up right in growth and the plant makes an excellent specimen or screen and is free berrying if pollinated by a suitable male.

Ilex aquifolium 'Handsworth New Silver'

A female clone of the 'argenteo marginata' group with purple stems and deep green leaves mottled with grey and with a broad creamy white margin. Produces ample red berries if pollinated by a male clone.

Ilex aquifolium 'J. C. van Tol'

A very beautiful holly with shiny, green leaves having almost no spines. It regularly **produces a large crop of red fruits, being self fertile**. It makes a compact,broad shrub.

Ilex aquifolium 'Pyramidalis'

A vigorous female form of holly, **producing masses of bright red berries and requiring no pollinator**. The form is conical when young, broadening with maturity. The foliage is a glossy dark green, with both spiny and smooth leaves on the same plant. Can be used for hedging.

Ilex aquifolium 'Silver Milkboy'

A lovely cultivar with very spiny leaves which are dark green with a blotch of creamy white at the center. A male clone. Any green shoots must be cut out immediately or the plant will revert to all green.

Ilex aquifolium 'Silver Queen'

A very striking shrub with blackish purple young shoots, and broad, dark green leaves, marbled grey and bordered creamy white. A male form which does not produce berries.

Ilex crenata 'Golden Gem'

A gem of a shrub, as the name suggests. Dwarf, compact, evergreen, with small yellow leaves. Ideal for small gardens, in rockeries or with conifers and heathers.

Ilex myrtifolia

An unusual form of holly with small, glossy leaves, long, narrow and elegantly spined. It has a compact habit and red berries will form if a male holly is nearby.

Ilex verticillata

A deciduous holly which is probably self fertile (ie. requires no pollinator). It will make an impressive specimen tree and the stems are particularly good for Christmas decorations, with their masses of bright red berries. The young leaves in spring are tinged purple and the foliage turns yellow in autumn.Will not tolerate limey soils.

Ilex x altaclarensis 'Camelliifolia'

This is a self fertile holly with large, almost spineless leaves of shiny dark green. It has large bright red fruits .The plant is pyramidal in habit and has purple stems.

Ilex x altaclarensis 'Golden King'

This holly is high on my list of top ten shrubs. Evergreen with green and bright yellow margined leaves. Produces red berries in autumn and winter. Can be planted as a colourful hedge.

Indigofera gerardiana

An easy to please shrub, producing purplish pink flowers continously throughout the summer and autumn. It has elegant foliage and **thrives in dry, sunny conditions**.

Itea virginica

A small, attractive, erect branched shrub producing upright racemes of fragrant, creamy white flowers in July. **Good autumn tints**.

Jasminum nudiflorum

A beautiful and tolerant, winter flowering shrub or climber. Bright yellow flowers appear on the green stems from November to February. **Excellent for covering walls and banks and training against fences.**

Juniperus 'Grey Owl'

A vigorous, wide spreading shrub. The foliage is soft silvery grey, **makes excellent ground cover** for a large rock garden or to cover banks.

Juniperus chinensis 'Aurea'

A golden cultivar of the Chinese Juniper which holds its colour well in the winter. It is conical in shape but may take a while to form a leader. **Ideal for garden in full sun.**

Juniperus chinensis 'Blue Point'

A new variety from the United States. Informal in habit, making more of a bush than a tree, with steel blue foliage.

Juniperus chinensis 'Kuriwao Gold'

A very hardy variety making a very bushy plant with distinctive upright branching habit. The foliage is dense and golden green. Ideal for conifer and heather beds.

Juniperus chinensis 'Pyramidalis' ('Stricta')

One of the bluest junipers, making a perfect pyramid shape if planted in an open position. A good contrast with heathers and other conifers.

Juniperus chinensis 'Robusta Green'

A juniper with informal upright habit and ideal as an accent plant or in the heather garden where its dense, bright green foliage will make an impressive contrast.

Juniperus communis 'Compressa'

A real gem of a dwarf conifer. It forms a tight conical bush, grey green in colour. **A must in any rock garden**, even small enough for a sink garden.

Juniperus communis 'Depressa Aurea'

In spring and summer this conifer is brilliant butter yellow, in autumn and winter it turns bronze. Good ground cover. For best colour grow in full sun.

Juniperus communis 'Hibernica'

The Irish Juniper forms a narrowly conical tree with a silvery sheen to the dark green foliage. In its best form it makes a slender column and is excellent accent plant either as a specimen or in a large heather garden. It may tend to open up with age and need tying.

Juniperus communis 'Repanda'

A fine mat forming juniper, making a dense carpet of dull green which bronzes slightly in winter.

Juniperus communis 'Wallis'

An upright, bushy juniper with grey foliage, prickly to the touch. **Very easy to please**.

Juniperus conferta

A superb ground cover juniper. The foliage is bright apple green. While it looks soft, it is in fact quite prickly. Makes a good contrast with darker conifers.

Juniperus horizontalis 'Blue Chip' (**'Blue Moon'**)

An outstanding ground cover plant with brilliant, soft silver blue foliage all summer, blue grey in winter.

Juniperus horizontalis 'Emerald Spreader'

A really ground hugging juniper with attractive emerald green foliage. **Excellent for covering banks**.

Juniperus horizontalis 'Glauca'

This is a real ground hugging plant and could even be used as a 'lawn'. It has numerous branches like whip-cord and the foliage is steel-blue in colour. Excellent for covering banks.

Juniperus horizontalis 'Hughes'

One of the best prostrate junipers with slightly raised foliage of a glowing silver.

Juniperus horizontalis 'Plumosa Compacta'

The foliage is feathery, grey green, purplish in winter. Semi prostrate habit, good ground cover.

Juniperus horizontalis 'Plumosa Youngstown'

A semi prostrate juniper with bright grey green foliage, purple bronze in winter. Excellent ground cover and **very easy to please**.

Juniperus horizontalis 'Winter Blue'

A semi prostrate juniper with blue green foliage soft to the touch. Ideal for the large rockery and ground cover for a difficult spot in the garden.

Juniperus procumbens 'Nana'

A real gem of a juniper. Completely prostrate and will shape itself over rocks etc. Apple green foliage and very dense habit.

Juniperus sabina 'Blue Danube'

A low growing juniper with spreading branches and grey green foliage.

Juniperus sabina 'Rockery Gem'

An attractive ground cover Juniper with silvery blue grey foliage. It is a vigorous and spreading variety, ideal for the larger rockery or on banks.

Juniperus sabina 'Tamariscifolia'

A very old and popular juniper, making a very attractive plant building up slowly with age, the branches overlapping each other. Excellent ground cover on banks and trailing over a wall.

Juniperus scopulorum 'Blue Heaven'

An outstanding form of the 'Rocky Mountain Juniper' with bright, silvery blue foliage all year round. The form is strongly pyramidal which makes this conifer a **good specimen plant** for the conifer and heather garden.

Juniperus scopulorum 'Blue Pyramidal'

An upright growing juniper with blue grey foliage and very narrow habit. An ideal specimen plant or with heathers and conifers.

Juniperus scopulorum 'Skyrocket'

Perhaps the narrowest, most pencil like of all conifers, with grey green foliage. A superb specimen plant ideal for conifer and heather beds.

Juniperus scopulorum 'Table Top Blue'

A spreading form of the Rocky Mountian Juniper with blue foliage turning a brilliant blue in the summer. The habit is semi prostrate and is improved by occasional trimming of the leading shoots.

Juniperus squamata 'Blue Carpet'

A top ten conifer with brilliant blue foliage all year round, just dulling slightly in winter. Excellent ground cover, good for heather and conifer beds, **looks brilliant on a sunny bank**.

Juniperus squamata 'Blue Star'

We think this is one of the most beautiful dwarf conifers. It has a compact habit with vivid blue foliage sometimes tingeing purple in winter. Will give a great deal of pleasure in your garden.

Juniperus squamata 'Meyeri'

A fine blue juniper making a bush of irregular habit. Needs yearly pruning to keep it an attractive plant.

Juniperus taxifolia 'Lutchuensis'

This variety we feel will become one of the most popular Junipers. It has apple green foliage and hugs the ground, **deal for trailing over walls** and down banks.

Juniperus virginiana 'Burkii'

A very upright column of dense, steel blue foliage in summer, turning bronze purple in winter. This conifer should be planted more often as it makes a **first class specimen**.

Juniperus virginiana 'Helle'

An attractive conifer with rather plume like, green foliage. A well shaped plant that makes an ideal specimen, good with heathers and other conifers.

Juniperus virginiana 'Silver Spreader'

An outstanding ground cover variety with shining grey summer foliage. Ideal with other conifers and heathers. **Will tolerate dry conditions** once established.

Juniperus x davurica 'Expansa Aureospicata'

A semi prostrate Juniper, the rich green foliage has splashes of gold. **Ideal for planting on banks** as ground cover, or with other conifers as contrast.

Juniperus x media 'Gold Coast'

This outstanding semi prostrate juniper retains its golden colour well in winter. Very dense bushy habit.

Juniperus x media 'Mint Julep'

One of the finest junipers for ground cover, its mint green foliage looking superb throughout the year.

Juniperus x media 'Old Gold'

This is becoming one of our most popular junipers, with its semi prostrate habit, holding its gold colour well in winter. More suited to the smaller garden than 'Pfitzerana Aurea' as the latter becomes fairly large.

Juniperus x media 'Pfitzerana Aurea'

An outstanding variety, excellent ground cover for the larger garden. The tips of the branches turn from yellow green in winter, to golden yellow in early summer.

Juniperus x media 'Pfitzerana Glauca'

A semi prostrate juniper with grey glaucous foliage. **Will tolerate almost any conditions**. Ideal to cover unsightly banks and difficult areas.

Juniperus x media 'Pfitzerana'

This vigorous, semi prostrate juniper wil tolerate almost any conditions. Individual plants vary in habit from tree like to prostrate.

Juniperus x media 'Plumosa Aurea'

A very beautiful form of juniper. The foliage is a bright golden yellow in summer, turning to bronze gold in winter. The branches are fairly upright, arching at the tips.

Juniperus x media 'Sulphur Spray'

A semi prostrate juniper with a difference. It has a whitish appearance all winter, brighter during the summer months and making a brilliant feature in the conifer and heather garden.

Kalmia augustifolia 'Rubra'

A small, evergreen shrub producing deep rosy red flowers in June and July. Very much like the rhododendrons needing peaty conditions and semi shade.

Kalmia latifolia

A magnificent, rhododendron like shrub, with pink flowers in June and rich, glossy foliage. Needs acid soil and semi shade.

Kerria japonica

A very easy shrub to grow, with arching branches and bright yellow flowers in April and May. Green stems also add to the interest of the shrub.

Kerria japonica 'Pleniflora'

A well known, double, yellow flowered shrub with green stems. **Will grow in most conditions**.

Kerria japonica 'Variegata' ('Picta')

An easy to please shrub with creamy white variegated foliage and single yellow, buttercup like flowers in April and May. Attractive green stems.

Kolkwitzia amabilis

A lovely and graceful, hardy shrub. Its drooping branches are draped with masses of bell shaped, pink flowers in May and June.

Laburnum alpinum 'Pendulum'

A slow growing form of the Scotch Laburnum which develops a low dome shaped head. The long racemes of golden yellow flowers hang from the pendulous branches in early June. It comes from the Southern Alps of Europe where it grows in damper soils than the Common Laburnum. Despite its common name it is not a native of the British Isles.

Laburnum x watereri 'Vossii'

This lovely plant is available in tree and bush form. It produces lovely racemes of yellow pea flowers. Most parts of this plant are poisonous, particularly the seeds, though 'Vossii' does not produce much seed.

Larix decidua

A fast growing, deciduous tree with light green foliage all summer, turning yellow in autumn. A very beautiful tree but only for larger gardens.

Larix kaempferi 'Pendula'

A weeping form of the Japanese Larch, making a beautiful tall and elegant tree with long drooping branches. This deciduous conifer is more vigorous when young than its European counterpart but less large when mature. The winter shoots are reddish brown and its summer foliage sea green, turning yellow at leaf fall. Often known as L.leptolepis.

Lavandula 'Hidcote'

A well known dwarf evergreen, compact in habit, producing dense spikes of violet flowers from late July. Pruning each spring produces the best results. **Fragrant foliage**.

Lavandula 'Munstead'

A compact growing lavender with narrow green leaves. Blue spikes of flowers appear from July. Prune hard each spring to keep plant compact.

Lavandula 'Vera'

A robust form of Lavender with broad, silver grey leaves. Lavender blue flowers appear in summer. **Makes an attractive low hedge**.

Lavatera olbia

A vigorous shrub with large, pink, saucer shaped flowers from late June to October. The foliage is soft, downy grey. Prune hard each spring. If in an exposed position take a third of the wood off in autumn.

Leucothoe fontanesiana 'Rainbow'

A little known evergreen which **thrives in shady conditions** and acidsoil. The foliage changes colour during the year and at times shows all these colours: green, cream, yellow and pink. White, pitcher shaped flowers appear in May.

Leycesteria formosa

A medium sized shrub with hollow green stems and white flowers in dense, terminal, drooping panicles of claret coloured bracts, appearing from June to September, followed by large, shining reddish purple berries.

Ligustrum japonicum 'Rotundifolium'

A very slow growing, dwarf shrub with black green, rounded leaves. **A collector's shrub**.

Ligustrum ovalifolium

The well known privet is easy to please. It is mainly used for hedging, and only in very bad winters does it lose its leaves.

Ligustrum ovalifolium 'Argenteum'

The silver privet can be used as a shrub or for hedging. The leaves are green with creamy white margins.

Ligustrum ovalifolium 'Aureum'

A brightly coloured privet with rich yellow, green centred leaves, often completely yellow. Makes an attractive shrub or hedging plant.

Lonicera fragrantissima

A valuable garden plant for its **early, charming fragrant blossom**. The retention of the leaves depends upon the severity of the winter but it is seldom defoliated. The cream-coloured flowers are produced in late winter and spring, followed in May by red berries. Introduced by Robert Fortune in 1845.

Lonicera nitida

A dense evergreen shrub suitable for hedging, quick growing and responds well to clipping. The leaves are small, ovate and glossy dark green. Small yellow-green flowers appear in April and May followed by semi translucent violet berries.

Lonicera nitida 'Baggessen's Gold'

This plant belongs to the Honeysuckle family. The tiny gold leaves brighten up the garden summer and winter. **Best in a sunny position**, can also be used as screening.

Lonicera pileata

A dwarf, semi evergreen shrub, horizontally branched, excellent ground cover. The leaves are small and bright green, violet berries appear in autumn.

Magnolia 'Suzan'

A new variety of Magnolia, compact habit like Stellata, with large, tulip shaped flowers of rich purple. This will become a much sought after plant in the future.

Magnolia grandiflora

This is certainly one of the most handsome evergreen flowering shrubs, which is very successful against a wall. It can be seen well established in the colleges of Oxbridge Universities. The very large cup shaped flowers are creamy-white and produce a fragrance throughout the summer and early autumn. The large leathery leaves are dark glossy green and reddish-brown beneath. A superb specimen plant in a sheltered position.

Magnolia grandiflora 'Exmouth'

A magnificent evergreen with large glossy leaves, often reddish beneath. Very large, creamy white, fragrant flowers appear in late summer and autumn. Best grown as wall shrub.

Magnolia liliiflora 'Nigra'

A wide spreading shrub with shiny, dark green leaves. The flowers are creamy white, stained purple, produced from April to June.

Magnolia sieboldii

Makes a large and wide spreading shrub with large oblong leaves dark green above and glaucous beneath. The flowers are fragrant, cup shaped and white. The stamens form a disk of maroon crimson in the centre of the flower. The blooms are borne intermittently from May to August. Introduced from Japan and Korea by Messrs Veitch about 1879. Award of Garden Merit 1935.

Magnolia stellata

A charming Japanese magnolia, slow growing and ideal for the smaller garden. White, star shaped flowers appear in March and April. Can also be grown in a large tub.

Magnolia stellata 'Rosea'

An outstanding variety. Small, pale pink, star shaped flowers appear in spring. **The compact habit makes it ideal for the smaller garden.**

Magnolia x proctoriana

A hybrid between M. salicifolia and M.stellata introduced in 1928. The plant forms a large shrub or small tree, and is very free flowering with six to twelve petalled blooms in April. The new growths are covered with silky hairs.

Magnolia x soulangiana

This is the most popular magnolia, with large, tulip shaped flowers, white, stained rose purple at the base, appearing before the leaves.

Magnolia x soulangiana 'Rustica Rubra'

One of the best of the Soulangiana Magnolias with rich rosy red cup shaped flowers. The plant is vigorous with bright green foliage, and received an Award of Garden Merit, R.H.S in 1969.

Mahonia 'Charity'

A superb, autumn and winter flowering, evergreen shrub. The fragrant, deep yellow racemes of flowers appear during autumn and early winter.

Mahonia aquifolium

An easy to please evergreen with polished green leaves, sometimes turning red in autumn. Rich yellow flowers open in early spring, followed by blue black berries. A very decorative shrub, **excellent ground cover**.

Mahonia aquifolium 'Apollo'

The glossy green foliage tints crimson purple in winter, and the yellow flowers in spring are followed by bluish black berries.

Mahonia aquifolium 'Moseri'

This is a very interesting shrub, as all its new foliage is bronze red, holding that colour over a long period. It produces yellow flowers in March and April followed by blue black berries.

Mahonia bealei

A fine, winter flowering evergreen with erect racemes of fragrant, yellow flowers between December and March. Can be planted in a large tub.

Mahonia japonica

This is rightly one of the top ten shrubs. Evergreen and from autumn to early spring, bearing terminal clusters of pendulous, scented, yellow flowers.

Malus 'John Downie'

The flowers are white, the fruits are quite large, bright orange and red, of conical shape and refreshing flavour.

Malus floribunda

Very beautiful when in flower, crimson buds open to white, to blush pink, followed by small, red and yellow fruits. One of the earliest crabs to flower.

Metasequoia glyptostroboides

Makes an outstanding specimen for the large garden, and one of the few deciduous conifers. It has feathery, plume like foliage and a lovely conical habit in time.

Microbiota decussata

This conifer is proving a real winner. Very low growing and with densely packed, lacy foliage, rich green in summer, bronzing in winter. The colour change is quite startling.

Myrtus apiculata 'Glen Gleam'

A lovely evergreen species which in favourable conditions can make a small tree. This form has been recently introduced, and is notable for the leaves having irregular white margins and the young growth tinged pink. The typical plant has attractive peeling bark and fragrant flowers with golden yellow anthers. The leaves are aromatic. **Needs some protection**.

Myrtus communis

This small, aromatic, evergreen shrub needs a sheltered position. White flowers appear in July and August.

Myrtus communis 'Tarentina'

A delightful evergreen shrub with aromatic foliage. White flowers appear profusely in July and August, followed by white berries.

Nandina domestica

This plant resembles a bamboo but in fact is related to the berberis. The leaves are stained with red when young, maturing to pale green. In autumn they turn shades of purple. The white flowers in clusters may be followed by scarlet or white fruits which stay during the winter.

Nandina domestica 'Pygmaea'

A compact bamboo-like shrub, which is prehaps surprisingly a member of the Berberis family. The plant has lance shaped leaves tinged red in spring and becoming purplish-red in the autumn and grows to about 2 ft. high. It makes an interesting variation in form for the larger rock garden or the mixed border in full sun and a protected position.

Olearia haastii

A rounded, evergreen bush, smothered with fragrant, daisy like, white flowers in July and August. **Can also be used as a fragrant hedge**.

Olearia macrodonta

A strong growing, evergreen shrub with sage green, holly like leaves, silvery white beneath. White, fragrant flowers in broad panicles appear in June. **Can be used for hedging or screening**.

Osmanthus delavayi

A beautiful, small leaved evergreen, slow growing with fragrant white, jasmine like flowers freely produced in April.

Osmanthus heterophyllus 'Variegatus'

A slow growing, holly like shrub, often mistaken for holly. Leaves are spine toothed, bordered creamy white. Sweetly scented white flowers appear in autumn.

Osmarea 'Burkwoodii'

A first class evergreen shrub, compact of growth with white flowers in April and May. **Very fragrant**.

Pachysandra terminalis

A very useful carpeting evergreen, which thrives in shady conditions. Greenish white flowers appear in February and March.

Pachysandra terminalis 'Variegata'

This is the attractive variegated form of pachysandra. The grey green leaves are edged with white and are evergreen. Greenish white flowers appear in February, March. **Will not tolerate deep shade like the green form**.

Paeonia suffruticosa (arborea)

These are beautiful shrubs with enormous flowers, available in a range of colours, varying from white through pink, to deep crimson and scarlet, with single, semi double and fully double flowers. Though hardy, the tender spring shoots require protection from frost till they have hardened. The plants are best grown in a spot where the morning sun will not reach them after frost.

Parrotia persica

A large shrub that we think is one of the finest autumn colouring shrubs. The bark on older specimens flakes like the London Plane. Flowers consisting of a cluster of crimson stamens appear in March, though not of great value.

Pernettya mucronata

Small white flowers appear in May and June followed by berries in late summer and autumn. The shrub is also evergreen and makes good ground cover. For best results plant a male plant to pollinate the females. Berries are red, pink or white.

Pernettya mucronata (Male)

This dwarf evergreen with white flowers in May and June, is valuable for pollinating the female plants which produce berries.

Perovskia atriplicifolia 'Blue Spire'

A small shrub with aromatic grey foliage smelling of sage. Spikes of blue flowers appear in August and September.

Philadelphus 'Beauclerk'

A superb medium sized shrub. The single milk white flowers have a zone of light cerise around the stamens and are **very fragrant**.

Philadelphus 'Belle Etoile'

My favourite mock orange. The single white flowers are flushed maroon at the centre and are delightfully fragrant.

Philadelphus 'Manteau d'Hermine'

A mock orange of dwarf compact habit with very fragrant creamy white flowers borne in clusters of 3-5. This is one of the many hybrids made by Lemoine of Nancy, at the end of the last century and was introduced in 1898. A free flowering and neat shrub for sun or part shade and excellent for the smaller garden.

Philadelphus 'Virginal'

A tall, upright growing shrub with rich, fragrant, double white flowers in June and July.

Philadelphus coronarius 'Aureus'

A small shrub with bright yellow foliage when young, turning greenish yellow later. White, fragrant, single flowers appear in June and July. **For best foliage colour plant in semi shade**.

Philadelphus coronarius 'Variegatus'

A little known Mock Orange, producing fragrant white flowers. The foliage is variegated with a creamy white margin. An outstanding shrub.

Phlomis fruticosa

Bright yellow flowers in late summer. Medium sized grey, felty leaves. A good plant for a sunny bank. Received an Award of Garden Merit in 1929.

Phormium tenax

An imposing architectural plant forming wide clumps with sword-like leaves 6 to 9 feet long when suited. When established the plants produce a flower spike 5 to 15 feet high with a panicle of rusty red flowers. The leaves are green slightly glaucous with a reddish or orange line on the margins. Native of New Zealand and introduced in 1789 at Kew.

Phormium tenax 'Bronze Baby'

A dwarf form of the New Zealand Flax with sword shaped leaves deep coppery-bronze in colour and up to 2 feet in length. When established it will produce a tall flowering spike. An 'architectural' plant which **needs good drainage and sun**.

Phormium tenax 'Purpureum'

A spectacular specimen plant and ideal as an architectural feature in the shrub border. The sword-like leaves are up to 6 feet in length and purplish in colour and are held erect making an imposing clump. They can be damaged in a bad winter, but **can tolerate most soil conditions and situations**.

Phormium tenax 'Variegatum'

A handsome evergreen with sword like leaves with a creamy white margin. Ideal to contrast with conifers and heathers and first class in tubs. **Needs good drainage and a sunny position**.

Phormium tenax 'Yellow Wave'

A medium sized flax with sword shaped leaves, golden yellow edged in green. Excellent for a tub in sunny position. **A good 'accent' plant**.

Photinia glabra 'Rubens'

A choice selected form with brilliant red young leaves to rival Pieris Forest Flame. The evergreen Photinias are lime tolerant and make handsome large shrubs or even small trees at maturity. A native of Japan and China, this variety is of New Zealand origin where it has been cultivation since the 1930's. Only recently introduced to Britain. Award of Merit 1972.

Photinia x frazeri 'Red Robin'

A spectacular shrub, evergreen, with bright red new growth equal to Pieris 'Forest Flame', but quicker growing. **Can be used for quite startling screening**.

Phygelius capensis

A delightful small shrub from South Africa with semi evergreen foliage. Bright scarlet, tubular flowers with a yellow throat appear from July to October. **Can be grown as a wall shrub** but requires a trellis or similar support.

Picea abies

The tree we all know, the one that decorates our living rooms at Christmas. With so many beautiful conifers to choose from, best left as a forest tree.

Picea abies 'Frohburg'

This is **a real collector's plant**. Slender upright main stem, with all of its branches weeping down tightly against the stem, forming in time a rich green carpet at the base of the tree.

Picea abies 'Little Gem'

A slow growing, dwarf conifer with small densely packed leaves and bright new shoots in spring. Globular habit. Ideal for the rock garden.

Picea abies 'Nidiformis'

An outstanding small spruce, flat topped with dark green foliage and attractive winter buds. The new growth is very light, fresh green.

Picea brewerana

One of the most beautiful conifers of all, but takes a few years to see it at its best, when it forms a broad conical tree, its branches clothed with long pendulous branchlets of dark blue green.

Picea glauca 'Alberta Globe'

A real gem forming a globe of light green, quite startling in spring with its new growth. Ideal for rockery and conifer bed.

Picea glauca 'Albertiana Conica'

High on any top ten conifer list, this plant has a perfect cone shape, slow growing with attractive, bright green foliage in spring. A gem for the rock garden and heather bed. Spray each spring against red spider.

Picea mariana 'Ericoides'

This is a dwarf form with blue grey leaves, soft to the touch. It is semi prostrate and should prove a real winner.

Picea mariana 'Nana'

A dwarf variety of the black spruce, very difficult to obtain. It forms a tightly congested ball of blue grey, with the blue predominant in summer.

Picea omorika

This spruce looks very much like our common Christmas tree, but in our opinion it is far better. The foliage is rich green above, glaucous beneath. The cones are conical in shape and bluish black. **A tree for the larger garden**.

Picea omorika 'Nana'

A very slow growing form of Serbian Spruce, with a compact rounded habit in early days, conical with age. The foliage is light green above with blue green bands beneath. A fine specimen for the conifer or heather garden.

Picea orientalis 'Aurea' (**'Aureospicata'**)

To many of us this conifer looks like a Christmas tree for most of the year. However, when established in a sunny position the new growth is quite startling, bright gold on top of all the branches, fading to green in late summer.

Picea pungens 'Globosa'

One of the finest dwarf conifers of all. Brilliant blue foliage and a rounded compact habit. Ideal for the rock garden, heather and conifer garden.

Picea pungens 'Hoopsii'

One of the bluest of the spruces, forming a magnificent conical specimen tree in time. The leading shoot needs training up straight in early years.

Picea pungens 'Koster'

This cone shaped conifer forms a fine specimen tree with bright blue foliage. Needs staking and training up straight in its early years.

Picea pungens 'Moerheimii'

One of the most beautiful blue spruces, forming a dense conical tree of vivid blue. Takes time to fill out and make impact, but well worth the wait.

Pieris 'Forest Flame'

For me, one of the finest shade loving evergreens. New growth is brilliant red, changing to pink and creamy white, finally to green. White, lily of the valley flowers appear in spring.

Pieris formosa forestii

This is one of the most beautiful of all shrubs. The young foliage is brilliant red and clusters of large white, slightly fragrant flowers appear in April and May.

Pieris formosa forrestii 'Wakehurst'

A very beautiful selected form of P.f. Forrestii, strong growing with vivid red young foliage contrasting with the glistening white flowers like lily of the valley. The leaves are comparatively large and broader than the type. The early growth is very susceptible to spring frosts and should be protected from the early morning sun. **A very desirable plant for a semi shade position in acid soil.**

Pieris japonica

A very fine evergreen with copper coloured foliage in spring and white, lily of the valley flowers in April and May in drooping clusters. **Needs acid soil.**

Pieris japonica 'Purity'

This outstanding, shade loving evergreen is in my top ten shrubs. Compact habit, bronze new growth in spring and large trusses of snow white flowers in spring. **Needs acid soil.**

Pieris japonica 'Variegata'

A slow growing shrub, leaves prettily variegated with creamy white, flushed pink when young. White, lily of the valley flowers appear in spring.

Pieris japonica (seedling)

This is a new seedling form of pieris. It has a much more compact habit than P. japonica and is slower growing. White, lily of the valley flowers open in spring from pink buds. Grows best in semi shade or shade in lime free soil.

Pieris taiwanensis

A very beautiful evergreen which thrives in peaty, shaded conditions. Young growth is coppery bronze and clusters of white flowers appear in March and April.

Pinus aristata

This is reputed to be the longest living plant in the world. In parts of theU.S.A. there are plants said to be over 5,000 years old. The plant has bluish green foliage that has the appearance of being covered with resinous white spots, which though unique, may not be considered by some to be particularly attractive.

Pinus mugo

A pine from the mountains of Central Europe, which is very variable in its habit. In its typical form it makes a low, bushy and spreading shrub up to 6 ft. high. The needles are vivid green, up to 3 inches long and set in pairs. **It will grow in the poorest of soils**.

Pinus mugo 'Humpy'

A very compact form of the 'Mountain Pine', good for rockeries and tubs. Makes a dense, rounded bush with short green needles.

Pinus mugo 'Mops'

An outstanding dwarf pine of compact habit with green foliage. Ideal for the rockery, conifer and heather beds.

Pinus mugo 'Ophir'

A very rare and beautiful dwarf pine, attractive the year round. It has a compact round form and golden tinged foliage. Needs time to show how beautiful it is.

Pinus nigra

This plant becomes a large tree with age but is well worth a place in the larger garden. It has a dense habit with deep green foliage, makes a good wind break, withstanding poor conditions quite well.

Pinus parviflora 'Glauca'

An outstanding Japanese pine with irregularly placed branches with blue grey needles, and cones while still young. Ideal for the conifer or heather garden.

Pinus parviflora 'Tempelhof'

A very select conifer with upright habit and blue green foliage. The branches are irregularly placed and as a young tree, rather sparse.

Pinus strobus 'Nana'

A beautiful dwarf conifer with compact habit and blue green needles. Makes a fine contrast with other conifers and with heathers. **Outstanding new growth in spring**.

Pinus sylvestris

The common pine, grown as a forest tree but in large gardens makes a fine specimen. It has grey blue foliage and reddish bark.

Pinus sylvestris 'Aurea'

One of the collectors' conifers, golden yellow needles all winter, yellow green in summer. A must for the heather garden. A plant that has to be grafted which makes it fairly expensive.

Pinus sylvestris 'Nana'

A slow growing pine with rounded habit and grey green needles. Makes a fine contrast with other conifers and heathers.

Pinus sylvestris 'Watereri'

A strong growing bush, conical at first, rounded with age, the foliage is blue green. **Excellent on a large rockery** or conifer and heather bed.

Pinus wallichiana 'Griffithii'

A beautiful pine eventually making a large, broad headed tree. It has soft blue needles and is quite startling in spring with new growth. Holds its lower branches well.

Pittosporum tenuifolium

A charming evergreen with pale green leaves, prettily set on black twigs. Flowers, small, chocolate purple and honey scented appear in spring. **Used by flower arrangers a great deal**.

Pittosporum tenuifolium 'Arundel Green'

A superb evergreen shrub with small, rich green leaves on upright branches. Chocolate purple, honey scented flowers appear in spring. **An ideal tub plant**.

Pittosporum tenuifolium 'Garnettii'

A very fine variegated evergreen with green and white, pink flushed leaves. **Can be used for flower arranging**.

125

Pittosporum tenuifolium 'Purpureum'

A very interesting evergreen shrub, upright growing with pale green leaves in summer, turning bronze purple in winter. Small chocolate purple, honey scented flowers appear in spring, but this is mainly a foliage plant.

Pittosporum tenuifolium 'Silver Queen'

An outstanding, variegated evergreen with silver grey leaves which contrast with the black stems. **Can be cut for flower arranging**.

Pittosporum tenuifolium 'Tom Thumb'

A dwarf form of P.Tenuifolium Purpureum, which makes a compact small evergreen bush, having green leaves in summer turning to bronze-purple in winter. The small honey scented flowers are rather insignificant. Like all the Pittosporums it can be susceptible to severe cold. Plant in a sheltered spot.

Potentilla arbuscula

A long flowering shrub with large, rich yellow flowers from late June to October. **Easy to please**.

Potentilla dahurica 'Abbotswood'

A dwarf shrub with a very long flowering period: producing its white flowers from June to October. **Ideal for large rockeries**, covering sunny, dry banks or in a shrubbery.

Potentilla dahurica 'Hersii'

A small, free flowering shrub of erect habit, producing white flowers in abundance from June to October.

Potentilla x fruticosa 'Daydawn'

This variety should be more widely planted. The cream, pink tinged, buttercup shaped flowers are produced throughout the summer.

Potentilla x fruticosa 'Elizabeth'

A magnificent shrub producing rich, canary yellow flowers from June to October. As well as planted in a shrubbery it can be used for hedging.

Potentilla x fruticosa 'Golddigger

A very colourful shrub, which from June until September is a mass of golden yellow flowers.

Potentilla x fruticosa 'Goldfinger'

One of the many varieties of this outstanding shrub. Bright yellow, buttercup like flowers are produced from June to Sept.

Potentilla x fruticosa 'Katherine Dykes'

This long flowering shrub produces its primrose yellow flowers from June to October. A good variety for hedging.

Potentilla x fruticosa 'Klondike'

A shrubby Potentilla with deep bright yellow flowers and attractive foliage.An excellent small shrub, for a sunny position in the shrub border or large rock garden, which reaches a height of about 4 feet with a similar spread. It can be trimmed in spring to keep a compact shape.

Potentilla x fruticosa 'Longacre'

A dense growing, dwarf shrub producing large, sulphur yellow flowers all summer and into autumn.

Potentilla x fruticosa 'Primrose Beauty'

A small, spreading shrub with primrose coloured flowers from June to October. **Ideal for a small, informal hedge**.

Potentilla x fruticosa 'Princess'

A new variety of potentilla with delightful pink flowers appearing from early summer right through to November. The flowers have their best colour when in semi-shade, when in strong sun they may turn white.

Potentilla x fruticosa 'Red Ace'

Red flowers appear from June to October. Habit is compact and low growing. To hold the best flower colour, plant in semi shade. Can be planted as a small hedge.

Potentilla x fruticosa 'Royal Flush'

A recent introduction with rose pink flowers with golden centres produced from June to October. Good compact habit.

Potentilla x fruticosa 'Sunset'

One of the truly outstanding potentillas. The flower colour varies from deep orange to brick red. It holds its colour best in partial shade. **Can be used as a small hedge**.

Potentilla x fruticosa 'Tangerine'

A dwarf, wide spreading shrub with pale coppery yellow flowers all summer. The flowers hold their unusual colour best when grown in semi shade.

Prunus 'Cistena'

A beautiful, red leaved shrub with white flowers in spring on bare twigs. Makes a lovely hedge as well as a good shrub.

Prunus 'Kanzan'

This is one of the showiest double pink flowering cherries. Upright when young, spreading with age. Young leaves are coppery red or reddish brown. Also available as a standard tree.

Prunus cerasifera 'Nigra'

A superb, strong growing shrub. The leaves and stems are blackish purple. Flowers of white fading to pink appear in March and April. **Excellent as a hedging plant**.

Prunus cerasifera 'Pissardii'

A superb, purple red leaved plum which produces white flowers from pink buds in March and April.

Prunus laurocerasus 'Castlewellan'

A rather unusual laurel with creamy stripes on glossy green foliage.

Prunus laurocerasus 'Otto Luyken'

A low growing evergreen with shiny green leaves. White flowers appear inApril followed by black berries. **Good ground cover**, **even in dense shade**.

Prunus laurocerasus 'Rotundifolia'

In my opinion, this is the best screening and hedging laurel. It has broad, evergreen leaves and white flowers in spring.

Prunus lusitanica

A large evergreen shrub that makes a beautiful specimen plant. Small, white hawthorn scented flowers are carried in long slender racemes in June. Small red berries follow, eventually turning black. Good hedging and screening plant.

Prunus lusitanica 'Variegata'

A large, attractive evergreen shrub that makes a beautiful specimen plant. White margined leaves sometimes flushed pink in winter. The small, white, scented flowers are carried in long slender racemes in June. Small fruit of red turning to dark purple.

Prunus serrulata 'Amanogawa'

A very popular cherry with the same habit as a poplar tree. Semi double, blush pink flowers in April and May. Young leaves are bronze to green. **Ideal for a small garden**.

Prunus subhirtella 'Autumnalis Rosea'

There are both bush and tree forms of the winter flowering cherry. The pale pink flowers are produced intermittently from November to March. Ideal for cutting a few sprays for the house.

Prunus tenella

A charming dwarf almond with upright stems. Bright pink flowers appear in April. Good for the smaller garden.

Prunus tenella 'Fire Hill'

A selected clone of the Russian Almond with darker flowers than the type and introduced from the Balkans by Lady Martineau. It received an Award of Merit in 1959. A low growing bushy shrub 2ft to 4ft high. The dark rosy pink flowers are borne in twos or threes on the previous years shoots. In its native country small almond-like fruits are produced.

Prunus triloba

This flowering almond is available as tree and shrub. The large, double, rosette like, clear peach pink flowers appear in March and April. For best results prune back after flowering.

Punica granatum 'Nana'

A dwarf deciduous shrub for a sunny position in a sheltered rock garden. The funnel shaped flowers are brilliant orange scarlet and borne in profusion. The pomegranates only rarely bear fruit in our climate. The plant would be excellent in a cold conservatory and was granted an Award of Merit in 1936.

Pyracantha 'Golden Charmer'

A useful and attractive evergreen shrub that can be grown either as a freestanding specimen, a screening shrub or against a wall. White, hawthorn like flowers appear in spring followed by deep golden berries in large clusters.

Pyracantha 'Mohave'

A vigorous, evergreen shrub with glossy green leaves and white, hawthorn like flowers in May and June. Bright red berries last into winter. Good hedging, screening and wall plant as well as free standing shrub.

Pyracantha 'Orange Charmer'

A useful and attractive evergreen, grown as a shrub or against a wall or fence. White ,hawthorn like flowers appear in spring followed by deep orange berries. Upright habit.

Pyracantha 'Orange Glow'

A vigorous, evergreen shrub with glossy green leaves and white, hawthorn like flowers in May and June. Bright orange berries last into winter. Good hedging, screening and wall plant as well as free standing shrub.

Pyracantha 'Teton'

A vigorous, evergreen shrub with glossy green leaves and white, hawthorn like flowers in May and June. The yellow orange berries last into winter. Good hedging and screening plant as well as free standing shrub.

Pyracantha 'Yellow Charmer'

A useful and attractive evergreen, grown as a shrub or against a wall or fence. White hawthorn like flowers are followed by large cluster of deep golden berries.

Pyracantha 'Yellow Sun'

A fine evergreen shrub with white flowers in early summer, followed by yellow berries which hold well into winter. Ideal shrub for growing against a wall.

Pyracantha coccinea 'Harlequin'

A variegated evergreen with foliage mottled and edged pale cream, may tinge pink in winter. White hawthorn flowers appear in May and June, followed by crimson berries in autumn and winter. Attractive wall shrub. Very tolerant but leaf colour best in sun.

Rhododendron 'Gristede'

A dwarf hybrid Rhododendron with masses of lavender blue flowers, A neat bushy plant and ideal for the rock garden.

Rhododendron 'Aksel Olsen'

Blood red flowers on top of distinctive green foliage making a Christmas likedisplay. The plant is interesting in that the upper branches are strong and upright while the lower are prostrate and creep along the ground.

Rhododendron 'Albert Schweitzer'

One of the earlier flowering rhodos. Pink trumpet shaped flowers, each with a dark red blotch, appear in April or May.

Rhododendron 'America'

A medium growing hybrid Rhododendron of rather lax and spreading habit but exceptionally hardy. The flowers are borne in a compact truss and are a bright red which is slightly blue toned. Is probably best in full sun. Introduced about 1920 by M. Koster and Sons.

Rhododendron 'Antge'

A compact rhodo, ideal for the smaller garden and in tubs. The foliage is glossy and evergreen. Clusters of rich red flowers appear in May and June.

Rhododendron 'Baden Baden'

A compact, dwarf growing Rhododendron ideal for tubs as well as the heather, shrub and conifer border. Rich red, bell shaped flowers appear in June.

Rhododendron 'Bengal'

A dwarf rhodo. with large dark red, bell shaped flowers. Will suit the smallest garden and can also be used in tubs.

Rhododendron 'Blitz'

An attractive small shrub with dark green, evergreen leaves. Clusters of funnel shaped, deep red flowers appear in mid May. A good tub specimen.

Rhododendron 'Blue Diamond'

A semi-dwarf ever green shrub with rich blue/purple flowers in April. A hybrid between Rh.augustinii and Intrifast. The growth is dense and compact.

Rhododendron 'Blue Tit'

A charming dwarf shrub with tiny evergreen leaves. Clusters of lavender blue flowers appear in April/ May, intensifying with age. **Small enough to be grown in a rock garden and tubs**.

Rhododendron 'Bremen'

A dwarf Rhododendron with rich red, bell like flowers in spring. The habit is very compact and **ideal for tubs and underplanting** with larger varieties and Azaleas.

Rhododendron 'Britannia'

A superb shrub, slow in growth, compact habit with dense trusses of glowing crimson scarlet flowers. The handsome foliage sets off the flowers and resists strong winds well.

Rhododendron 'Caractacus'

A hybrid of R. catawbiense. Deeply veined medium sized leaves. Purplish red flowers appear in May. **Extremely hardy** with compact growth habit. Foliage inclined to yellow in full sun. First Class Certificate 1865.

Rhododendron 'Carmen'

A dwarf rhododendron of very compact habit. Beautiful bell shaped flowers of dark crimson appear in spring. Ideal for small gardens or the rock garden. Award of merit.

Rhododendron 'Cary Ann'

Cheery coral red flowers flare like a trumpet bell. Beautiful foliage throughout the year. Its mature habit is a compact broad plant.

Rhododendron 'Chevalier Felix de Sauvage'

A fine evergreen with scarlet red, dark blotched flowers in May and June. Quite happy in shade or semi shade and peaty soil.

Rhododendron 'Chikor'

A dwarf Rhododendron of great merit awarded a First Class Certificate in 1968. It forms a compact little plant with masses of yellow flowers up to 6 in a truss in late April and early May every year. A cross between R. chryseum and R. ludlowii.

Rhododendron 'China Boy'

A small evergreen shrub with deep green leaves and clusters of clear red flowers from late April into May. **Good for tubs and the smaller garden**.

Rhododendron 'Cosmopolitan'

A hardy evergreen with deep pink flowers with a crimson blotch. **Ideal in semi shade**.

Rhododendron 'Cunningham's White'

An extremely hardy evergreen producing lax trusses of funnel shaped flowers, mauve pink in bud, opening white with a ray of pale purple and brown markings within.

Rhododendron 'Curlew'

One of the best dwarf rhododendrons. Very large yellow flowers on every shoot with dark green foliage. **Fairly compact habit**.

Rhododendron 'Cynthia'

A very hardy variety of rhododendron, forming a dome shaped bush, bearing magnificent conical trusses of rose crimson flowers with a narrow ray of blackish crimson markings within, appearing May and June.

Rhododendron 'Doncaster'

A slow growing, fairly dwarf Rhododendron, dome shaped in habit. Dense trusses of funnel-shaped, crimson scarlet flowers with a ray of black markings within. Very dark green, leathery foliage.

Rhododendron 'Dr. A.W. Endtz'

A fine evergreen with trusses of carmine flowers in May and June. Enjoys semi shade and being planted in lime free soil.

Rhododendron 'Dr. H.C. Dresselhuys'

A fine evergreen with rich green foliage and upright growth when young, spreading with age. Trusses of rich red flowers with yellow stamens appear in late May and June.

Rhododendron 'Dr. Tjebbes'

A good evergreen shrub for use under mature trees, where the clusters of red flowers are set off very well.

Rhododendron 'Dr. V.H. Rutgers'

An outstanding evergreen with rich green foliage and trusses of dark red, funnel shaped flowers. Ideal for woodland planting or semi shade, shady conditions. Plant in lime free soil.

Rhododendron 'Edward Rand'

A fine evergreen with dark green foliage and deep red trusses of flowers in May and June. **Ideal for shade or semi shade**.

Rhododendron 'Elizabeth'

An evergreen, dwarf rhododendron of spreading habit with rich dark red flowers carried in clusters in April.

Rhododendron 'Elsie Straver'

A campylocarpum hybrid of compact habit, with large bell shaped flowers creamy yellow with reddish brown eye. One of the best of the newer hardy yellow Rhododendrons and will probably grow to about 6 feet.

Rhododendron 'Everastianum'

One of the quicker growing rhododendrons. Dense habit with lilac flowers in June. Good screening plant as it is very hardy.

Rhododendron 'Fabia'

A beautiful cultivar with flat trusses of funnel shaped flowers. The colour is scarlet, shaded orange in the tube, and speckled with pale brown.

Rhododendron 'Fastuosum Flore Pleno'

A very hardy evergreen, forming a dome shaped bush. Rich mauve, funnel shaped flowers with a ray of crimson brown markings and wavy petal margins appear in lax trusses, from late May to June.

Rhododendron 'Golden Gate'

An evergreen shrub suitable for the smaller garden and in tubs. Orangey pink clusters of flowers appear in mid May.

Rhododendron 'Goldsworth Orange'

This forms a low spreading bush about 6 foot high and more across. The flowers are borne in a lax truss of up to 10 blooms, and are yellow tinged with pink, with a broad band of greenish brown speckles in the throat. Not one of the hardiest Rhododendron, but worthy of a sheltered position. A cross between R. dicroathum and R. discolor. Received an Award of Merit in 1959.

Rhododendron 'Gomer Waterer'

A hybrid of R. Catawbiense with white flowers, flushed pale mauve towards the edges, carried in large dense trusses. A vigorous evergreen shrub with large leathery leaves.

Rhododendron 'Harvest Moon '

A slow growing rhododendron of compact habit. The bell shaped flowers are a beautiful creamy colour with a crimson blotch. Award of Merit 1948.

Rhododendron 'Hugo Koster'

An excellent red large flowered hybrid, an improvement on Rh. Doncaster, which is one of its parents. Makes an upright and spreading bush with medium sized leaves. The flowers are borne in an upright truss and bright crimson red with a lighter centre.

Rhododendron 'Humming Bird'

A compact rhodo which forms a small dome. Flowering is early in the rhodo season, and the colour is carmine, shaded glowing scarlet inside wide, bell shaped blooms. Good for tubs or in a rock garden.

Rhododendron 'Jewel'

A dwarf rhododendron with shiny rounded leaves and clusters of red, trumpet shaped flowers in spring. This form is small enough for a rock garden, as well as in a tub.

Rhododendron 'John Walter'

An old hybrid Rhododendron of dense, bushy habit introduced by Waterers in 1860. The flowers are large, funnel shaped, bright crimson with brown markings and borne in a huge truss of up to 20 blooms. A very hardy cultivar, well worth a place in the garden. It flowers in early June.

Rhododendron 'Kate Waterer'

A fine evergreen with pink flowers which have a yellow blotch. Makes a fine specimen plant for lightly shaded areas.

Rhododendron 'Lady Clementine Mitford'

A large flowered hybrid Rhododendron with funnel shaped flowers peach-pink, paling to blush. An old hybrid which received an Award of Merit in 1971.

Rhododendron 'Lavender Girl'

A large flowered hybrid Rhododendron, a cross between Rhodo. fortunei and Lady Grey Egerton. The flowers are pale lavender and borne on a vigorous, but compact bush, with excellent foliage. **The flowers are fragrant**.

Rhododendron 'Linda'

A beautiful and compact dwarf rhododendron with rosy-red flowers borne in trusses of 7 or 8 . The leaves are oval in shape derived from its williamsianum parent. Bred in Boskoop, Holland from R. Brittania x R. williamsianum it received an award of Merit in 1968. **Excellent for a tub in part shade**.

Rhododendron 'Lord Roberts'

A fine hardy evergreen of erect habit. Flowers in dense rounded trusses, funnel shaped, dark crimson with black markings inside in May.

Rhododendron 'Madame Masson'

An extremly hardy rhododendron which has been known to survive 60 degrees of frost. Hybrid of R. ponticum and R. catawbiense. Very good habit with flowers of pure white with a yellow blotch.

Rhododendron 'Moerheim Pink'

An outstanding dwarf variety with bright pink bell flowers in spring. Ideal for planting in front of larger varieties. Can also go in tubs.

Rhododendron 'Moerheim'

A very dwarf rhodo with tiny green leaves and clusters of purplish blue flowers in spring. Suitable for tubs and very attractive on a rock garden.

Rhododendron 'Mrs T.H. Lowinsky'

A large flowered hybrid Rhododendron with flowers mauve in bud, opening mauve tinged fading to white. A free flowering and delightful plant which has Rhodos. ponticum and catawbiense in its blood. **Late flowering and can therefore extend the flowering season**.

Rhododendron 'Nova Zembla'

An evergreen shrub with rich green foliage and compact trusses of red flowers in May and June. Shade or semi shade in lime free soil are ideal conditions.

Rhododendron 'Osmar'

A Rhodo. Williamsianum hybrid with large flowers of rose to light lilac pink. The plant makes a bun shaped bush wider than tall. **It should not be planted in too much shade**.

Rhododendron 'Peter Koster'

A very handsome shrub, sturdy and bushy with firm trusses of trumpet shaped flowers in June. The petals are rosy crimson, paling towards the edge, darker in bud.

Rhododendron 'Pink Drift'

A very pretty dwarf shrub with tiny leaves and clusters of soft lavender rose flowers from May to mid June. Good for a rock garden or in tubs.

Rhododendron 'Pink Pearl'

One of the best known rhododendrons. Flowers are funnel shaped in large conical trusses, rose coloured in bud, opening to lilac pink, fading to white at the margins, with a well defined ray of crimson brown markings.

Rhododendron 'Prince Camille de Rohan'

A highly rated rhodo with a neat, compact habit. Clusters of light, rosy pink flowers, each with a dark red blotch appear in May or June.

Rhododendron 'Purple Pillow'

A dwarf hybrid Rhododendron with deep blue/purple flowers. It makes a neat cushion shaped bush and is free flowering. Probably a hybrid of Rhododendron impeditum.

Rhododendron 'Purple Splendour'

A slow growing and compact rhododendron, producing masses of flowers of rich purple with a strong black eye. Award of Garden Merit 1968.

Rhododendron 'Rose Ann Whitney'

A fine evergreen of compact habit with rose pink flowers in May and June. **Ideal for a tub**.

Rhododendron 'Roseum Elegans'

One of the faster growing rhodos but still making a neat, compact plant. Clusters of rose lilac flowers appear in May or June.

Rhododendron 'Sapphire'

A dwarf Rhododendron with small leaves and fairly open habit. Pale lavender blue flowers appear in April or early May.

Rhododendron 'Sappho'

A very free growing bush of rounded habit. Flowers in handsome conical trusses, mauve in bud, opening pure white with a conspicuous blotch of rich purple overlaid black.

Rhododendron 'Scarlet Wonder'

A very hardy dwarf shrub, forming a compact mound of dense foliage. The flowers are trumpet shaped, ruby red with frilly margins, borne in loose trusses at the shoots in late May and June.

Rhododendron 'Songbird'

A charming dwarf Rhododendron producing clusters of violet blue flowers in April. **Ideal for the rock garden**.

Rhododendron 'Unique'

A real gem of an evergreen, flower colour variously described as biscuit yellow, flushed apricot, or creamy white, tinged pink or flesh pink changing to buff. Very 'unique'. **Compact habit**.

Rhododendron 'Van Weerden Poelman'

An evergreen shrub with light red, funnel shaped flowers in late May and June. Ideal for semi shady or shady position in lime free soil.

Rhododendron 'Wilgens Ruby'

An outstanding evergreen with rich green foliage. Trusses of bright red, funnel shaped flowers appear in late May and June.

Rhododendron 'Winsome'

A Rhododendron hybrid of intermediate height raised by Lord Aberconway from Rh. griersonianum x Rh. Hummingbird. The large flowers are cherry pink and slightly speckled. The foliage is very attractive at all stages particularly the young growth which is copper coloured. A beautiful plant growing eventually to 6 feet. Award of Merit 1950.

Rhododendron brachycarpum

A fairly small rhodo producing white, pink flushed flowers in June and July. This means that it is much later flowering than most rhodos, and the display may be prolonged. The leaves have a fawn coloured fuzz underneath.

Rhododendron catawbiense

An extremely hardy evergreen with very large leaves. Flowers are borne in large trusses, bell shaped, varying in colour from lilac purple to pink or white and appearing in June. Ideal as a screening plant in lime free soil.

Rhododendron dichroanthum scyphocalyx

A small, slow growing rhodo with white or grey undersides to the leaves. The flowers appear in clusters, an unusual shade of coppery orange with red shading.

Rhododendron eudoxum

A small rhodo with soft pink flowers in clusters from the end of April into May. **Small enough for tubs and borders**.

Rhododendron fastigiatum

A small alpine variety of Rhododendron with tiny leaves and masses of purple flowers in April and May. An unusual addition to any rock garden.

Rhododendron fimbriatum

A dwarf rhodo with quite large clusters of bell shaped, violet mauve or purple flowers in April and May.

Rhododendron impeditum

A dwarf alpine shrub with tiny, grey green leaves. It forms a small mound and is covered with light purplish blue flowers in spring. **Ideal for the rockery**.

Rhododendron kiusianum

A delightful dwarf rhodo with evergreen or semi evergreen foliage, forming a dense, spreading mound. Clusters of flowers appear in May or June, the colour varying from salmon red to crimson or purple, but usually lilac purple.

Rhododendron lapponicum 'Hillier's Form'

A dwarf rhodo with dense, compact habit. Clear blue clusters of flowers appear in mid April. Good for tub or rockery work.

Rhododendron luteum (Azalea pontica)

A deservedly popular azalea which may occasionally be found growing wild. The yellow flower clusters appear in May or June and are very fragrant. The foliage turns rich shades of red, orange and yellow in autumn.

Rhododendron ponticum

This is the 'wild' rhododendron that makes such an eye catching display in peaty woodlands. The flowers are mauve to lilac pink, appearing in May or June. It is a useful plant for forming a large hedge or windbreak.

Rhododendron ponticum 'Variegatum'

An unusual rhododendron with leaves edged with a band of creamy white. Mauvey lilac pink flowers appear in May or June.

Rhododendron praecox

A charming dwarf shrub, one of the earliest rhododendrons to flower. Purplish crimson buds open to rosy purple flowers in Feb./March, appearing in twos and threes at the ends of the shoots. May lose some foliage in hard winters so is classed as semi evergreen.

Rhododendron punctatum

A small rhodo, good for tubs, which produces clusters of rosy purple flowers in May.

Rhododendron williamsianum

A very attractive rhodo from China. The leaves are smooth and oval, setting off the soft pink, bell shaped flowers that appear in April. **It has a generally dwarf, spreading habit**.

Rhododendron yakushimanum

A beautiful dwarf rhododendron from the Yakushima Island off Japan. It forms a compact dome shaped bush which carries a mass of bell shaped, blush pink to white flowers. The foliage is deep glossy green above and browm tomentose beneath.

Rhododendron x yakushimanum 'Bambi'

A dwarf rhodo with narrow, deep green leaves. The undersides of the leaves are covered in an orange tormentum (felt), and clusters of pale pink, darker spotted flowers appear in May or June.

Rhododendron x yakushimanum 'Bashful'

A dwarf rhododendron of compact rounded habit. Flowers are rose pink with reddish brown blotch. Good foliage.

Rhododendron x yakushimanum 'Chelsea Seventy'

A dwarf rhododendron of compact habit. Beautiful trusses of salmon shaded,rose pink flowers.

Rhododendron x yakushimanum 'Doc'

A dwarf rhododendron of compact habit. Large trusses of blush-pink flowers.

Rhododendron x yakushimanum 'Golden Torch'

A dwarf rhododendron of round tight habit. The flowers are salmon pink in bud opening to chrome yellow. Light green foliage.

Rhododendron x yakushimanum 'Hoppy'

A dwarf rhododendron with a wide spreading habit. Pale lilac flowers, fading to white when fully open.

Rhododendron x yakushimanum 'Pink Cherub'

A very pretty dwarf rhodo with a very compact habit. Large clusters of rose pink flowers with paler centres appear in late May, early June.

Rhododendron x yakushimanum 'Sneezy'

A dwarf rhododendron of compact rounded habit. The flowers are bright rose, deeper at the edge and with a dark red blotch. Good foliage.

Rhododendron x yakushimanum 'Titian Beauty'

A dwarf rhododendron of compact rounded habit. Bright crimson flowers and good tight foliage.

Rhododendron x yakushimanum 'Vintage Rose'

A dwarf rhododendron of compact habit. Large trusses of pink flowers, deeper pink in the centre. Good foliage, velvety brown beneath.

Rhus typhina

This small tree or large shrub is mainly grown for its brilliant autumn colour. Large, erect, green clusters of male flowers and smaller female clusters, are borne on separate plants, followed by dense, conical clusters of fruit.

Rhus typhina 'Laciniata'

A striking female form of this shrub, with deeply cut, fern like leaves which have rich autumn tints, and large conical seed pods of a dark crimson.

Ribes sanguineum 'King Edward VII'

This popular flowering currant with deep crimson flowers in April, can be used for hedging or the shrub border. Best to prune some of the old wood hard back after flowering each year.

Ribes sanquineum 'Pulborough Scarlet'

An easy to please shrub producing masses of deep red flowers in March and April.

Robinia hispida 'Rosea'

This little known shrub can be quite outstanding if planted in a sunny, well drained position. Rose pink flowers appear on short racemes in May and June. The branches are bristly and the foliage quite dainty and attractive.

Romneya coulteri

Large white, poppy like flowers with golden yellow stamens appear all summer. The stems and foliage are glaucous and the leaves are deeply cut. This plant can also be classed as a perennial as it dies down to ground level in winter.

Romneya x hybrida

Blue green, poppy like foliage is topped by sweetly scented white flowers which are six inches across. The central stamens are golden yellow and very conspicuous.

Rosmarinus officinalis

This plant can be used as a shrub as well as a herb. The foliage is greyish green, white beneath, with blue flowers in clusters along the branches in May.

Rubus tricolor

A very vigorous, evergreen ground cover plant with long trailing stems, covered with prickles. Inch wide white flowers appear in July, often followed by edible red fruits. **A very good plant for shady spots, even under trees**.

Ruta graveolens 'Jackman's Blue'

A striking form of this small evergreen with attractive, glaucous blue foliage and compact habit. Needs well drained soil and a sunny spot.

Salix hastata 'Wehrhahnii'

A slow growing shrub, which in spring becomes alive with pretty, silvery grey, male catkins on the stout twigs, turning yellow later.

Salix lanata

This is an attractive slow growing shrub. The rounded, mid green leaves are densely covered with grey white felt. Stout and erect catkins appear in March, April. **An unusual specimen for the rock garden**.

Salix sachalinensis 'Sekka'

A rather unusual shrub, which often has curiously flattened and recurved stems. These are encouraged by hard pruning. Green foliage, attractive catkins in spring.

Salvia officinalis 'Purpurascens'

A dwarf semi evergreen with stems and young foliage suffused purple. Particularly effective in coloured foliage groups for blending or contrast.

Sambucus racemosa 'Plumosa Aurea'

A very fine golden shrub with beautiful, deeply cut golden leaves. **Quite slow growing** and takes time to establish, so do not be disappointed if leaves scorch for one or two years, as in time you will be rewarded.

Santolina chamaecyparissus

A dwarf evergreen, mound forming with dense, silvery grey foliage and dainty, button like, yellow flowers in July. Prune hard in spring to retain good shape.

Sarcococca confusa

A small, spreading evergreen shrub with glossy leaves. The flowers have cream coloured anthers and are very fragrant. They are followed by shining black fruits.

Sarcococca humilis

A charming, dwarf evergreen with deep green leaves and small, white, very fragrant flowers in February and March. **Ideal for cutting for the house**. Black berries follow the flowers.

Senecio 'Sunshine' (greyi)

An attractive, silver grey evergreen, producing yellow flowers in July. Best pruned hard in spring to retain good shape.

Skimmia japonica 'Foremanii'

A small evergreen with broadly rounded leaves and white, fragrant flowers in April and May. Large bunches of brilliant red fruits follow in autumn and winter if a male form, ie Skimmia 'Rubella', is nearby.

Skimmia japonica 'Rubella'

High on my top ten list of shrubs. Evergreen, with red flower buds throughout the winter, opening in spring to white, fragrant flowers. The compact habit makes it a good shrub for tubs. **Will also tolerate heavy shade**. As well as being an ornamental shrub in its own right, it is also a pollinator for female forms such as 'Formanii'.

Skimmia reevesiana

A dwarf evergreen shrub forming a low mound. White flowers in May are followed by bright red berries which last right through the winter. This form of skimmia does not require a male to set the berries as it will set a full crop by itself.

Sophora japonica

This ultimately makes a medium to large sized tree. The ash-like foliage is made up of 9 to 15 leaflets. The flowers are creamy white,pea-like and born in large panicles but you must be very patient in expecting the tree to bloom. Originally from China but much planted in Japan and used for Bonsai.

Sorbaria aitchisonii

A vigorous shrub with ash like leaves and reddish young stems. Plumes of white flowers appear in July, August.

Spartium junceum

A sun loving shrub with yellow, fragrant, pea flowers summer and autumn. Best pruned hard in March, but not into old wood.

Spiraea cinerea 'Grefsheim'

A lovely compact form of the bridal wreath with arching habit. Masses of white flowers appear along the branches in April/May before the leaves.

Spiraea japonica 'Alpina'

A very useful dwarf and compact shrub for the smaller garden. Corectly named S. japonica 'nana' the flowers are lilac-pink and start to open earlier than the other varieties. A light clip over with shears in the Spring keeps the plant tidy. The plant is always wider than it is tall and can reach a width of 6 ft. when mature.

Spiraea japonica 'Gold Flame'

One of the finest spring foliage plants. The young growth is brilliant gold and flame coloured, turning light green later. Flat heads of pink flowers appear in summer.

Spiraea japonica 'Golden Princess'

Similar to 'Gold Flame' but more compact and retaining its gold foliage throughout the summer. The flat heads of bright pink flowers last for several weeks in midsummer. In the spring the young growth are tinged reddish bronze. A lovely shrub for the front of the border in full sun.

Spiraea japonica 'Little Princess'

A dwarf compact shrub forming a low mound, with rose crimson flowers from June to August.

Spiraea japonica 'Shirobana'

A new variety of Spiraea with pink and white flowers on the same plant. It is a small shrub, best kept to 12' or 15' in height by pruning hard in March.

Spiraea nipponica

A strong growing shrub with bushy, arching stems. The flowers are white, in clusters which crowd the upper branches in June. Each tiny flower is surrounded by a small green bract.

Spiraea nipponica tosaensis (Snowmound)

A dwarf compact shrub with branches smothered in white flowers in June.

Spiraea thunbergii

A popular shrub with a twiggy, spreading habit with white flowers along the branches in March and April. The foliage is an attractive light green.

Spiraea x arguta

When we see this lovely shrub in flower, we know that winter is over. The graceful, slender branches are covered with white flowers in April and May.

Spiraea x bumalda 'Anthony Waterer'

A dwarf shrub with bright crimson flowers carried on flat heads. The foliage is occasionally variegated. Prune hard in March to retain good shape.

Spiraea x vanhouttei

One of the finest white flowered spiraeas with gracefully arching branches carrying the dense clusters of small flowers along their length. A hybrid raised in France about 1862 and **very useful for forcing in to early bloom for flower arranging**. Very hardy and does best if the older wood is pruned out after flowering.

Stranvaesia davidiana

A vigorous evergreen shrub with white flowers in spring and clusters of red berries in autumn and winter. On established shrubs, the oldest leaves turn bright red, contrasting well with the young green leaves. Makes an excellent screening plant.

Stranvinia 'Redstart'

An exciting new evergreen plant. The new growth is coppery red, a few leaves are red all winter. Clusters of white flowers in June are followed by yellow tipped, red berries.A bigeneric hybrid between Stranvaesia and Photinia. Raised by Hilliers.

Symphoricarpos albus

One of the easiest shrubs to grow in most conditions, producing white berries which stay on the plant all winter. Small white flowers appear between June and August.

Symphoricarpos orbiculatus 'Variegatus'

A graceful plant with small leaves margined yellow, producing purplish pink berries. Will revert to green if planted in shade.

Symphoricarpos x doorenbosii

A strong growing shrub which produces white, pink tinged berries in autumn and winter. **Will grow in most conditions**. The flower is white and very small, appearing in June and July.

Symphoricarpos x doorenbosii 'White Hedge'

A small shrub that produces masse of white berries in autumn, lasting well into winter. This type is one of the best for hedging as it has tidy, upright growth. The flowers are small and white appearing in early summer. Easy to grow and tolerant of sun and shade, even under trees.

Syringa microphylla 'Superba'

An attractive, small leaved shrub with masses of fragrant, rose pink flowers in May, continuing intermittently until October.

Syringa microphylla 'Superba' (Standard)

A pretty, small leaved shrub which has masses of rose pink, fragrant flowers in May and intermittently until October.Grafted onto a small stem to make a small standard tree.

Syringa reflexa

A large shrub, flowers rich purplish pink outside, whitish within, densely packed in long narrow, drooping clusters, 6'-8' long in late May and June.

Syringa velutina (syn. palibiniana)

A very beautiful small shrub. A 'lilac' which can be planted in the larger rock garden and flowering in May and June with dense lilac pink panicles even on young plants. Introduced from Korea in 1910, it has unfortunately been plaqued by name changes. At one time known as S.palibiniana, it should now be correctly S.meyeri 'palibin'.

Syringa vulgaris 'Charles Joly'

This outstanding lilac has dark, purplish red, fragrant flowers in May or early June. No pruning needed except to take off dead flower heads in June.

Syringa vulgaris 'Katherine Havermeyer'

A first class lilac with fragrant, purple lavender, double flowers, fading to pale lilac pink, appearing in broad clusters in May or early June.

Syringa vulgaris 'Madame Lemoine'

One of the most outstanding lilacs, creamy yellow buds open to pure white,fragrant, double flowers in May or early June.

Syringa vulgaris 'Primrose'

A very unusual lilac with primrose yellow flowers in small, dense, fragrant clusters. We think this plant will be of great interest to the keen gardner.

Syringa x prestoniae 'Elinor'

A very hardy shrub, producing its dark, purplish red buds opening pale lilac, on current year's wood. Remove dead flowers as soon as possible.

Tamarix pentandra

The 'Tamarisk' forms quite a large shrub with delicate leaves. Bright pink flowers appear from July to September, clustered in short spikes, cascading from the arching branches.

Tamarix tetrandra

A large shrub with dark coloured branches and green foliage. Light pink flowers in slender racemes appear in May and early June on branches of the previous year.

Taxus baccata

This must be **one of the easiest to please conifers**. The foliage is very dark green, sometimes bronzing in winter. An ideal hedging plant, very neat growth, can be cut to almost any shape. Produces red berries which are poisonous.

Taxus baccata 'Dovastonii Aurea'

A wide spreading golden yew with branches arranged in tiers, drooping towards the ends. The foliage is margined gold.

Taxus baccata 'Fastigiata Aurea'

This makes a fine specimen, but is best planted with other conifers and heathers. It has an erect, narrow habit with bright gold foliage, dulling slightly in winter.

Taxus baccata 'Fastigiata'

A very erect growing, dark green conifer, staying very narrow for many years. Ideal for the conifer and heather garden.

Taxus baccata 'Semperaurea'

Possibly the best golden yew, forming a spreading bush bright gold in summer, old gold in winter. Ideal for the larger rock garden or conifer and heather bed.

Taxus baccata 'Standishii'

In my opinion one of the finest small growing conifers, with erect, upright habit, holding its golden foliage colour well all year. **A must for the heather and conifer garden**.

Taxus baccata 'Summergold'

This plant is semi prostrate with bright yellow foliage all summer, dulling slightly in winter. An ideal contrast whenplanted with heathers and conifers.

Teucrium fruticans

A small evergreen shrub needing a sunny, sheltered site. The leaves are grey green and the undersides and stems are white. Pale blue flowers are borne from June to September.

Thuja occidentalis 'Danica'

An outstanding dwarf variety forming a neat globe of dark green. Ideal for the conifer and heather bed.

Thuja occidentalis 'Golden Globe'

A fairly open, rounded habit. The foliage is rich gold, brighter summer than winter. We think this should become very popular.

Thuja occidentalis 'Holmstrup Yellow'

A beautiful slow growing dwarf conifer. In winter the bright golden yellow leaves shine out in a sunny position. The form is broadly pyramidal. Superb in the heather garden.

Thuja occidentalis 'Holmstrupii'

An outstanding variety forming a neat pyramid of rich green, bronzing slightly in winter if in an open position. Makes a fine specimen in the conifer and heather bed.

Thuja occidentalis 'Lutea Nana'

A very colourful conifer with golden foliage that is as good in winter as in summer. Quite slow growing, but in time makes a lovely specimen.

Thuja occidentalis 'Rheingold'

A very popular variety which varies a great deal in shape from plant to plant; sometimes a very round bush, sometimes conical. The colour of the foliage changes through the year; rich gold in summer, old gold with bronzing in winter. A must for the conifer and heather garden.

Thuja occidentalis 'Smaragd'

This conifer should be used a great deal more as a small hedge. It has very neat, upright growth, rich green, bronzing in winter. Very suitable for a spot where 'Leylandii' would be too vigorous.

Thuja occidentalis 'Sunkist'

Recently introduced from the Continent. A slow growing conifer of pyramidal habit with bright gold foliage throughout the year. **A plant of great merit**.

Thuja orientalis 'Aurea Nana'

An outstanding slow growing conifer, forming a small rounded bush. The foliage is brilliant gold in summer, bronze gold in winter.

Thuja orientalis 'Conspicua'

Probably the best form of Thuja orientalis for maintaining the colour of its golden yellow foliage. It forms a narrow conical tree of medium growth rateand needs a position in full sun to retain its colour.

Thuja plicata

A large, fast growing conifer with bright green, glossy foliage which has a very pleasant aroma when crushed. With age, this tree has cinnamon red or brown, shredding bark. It **makes an excellent hedging and screening conifer**.

Thuja plicata 'Atrovirens'

An outstanding variety for hedging and screening, with a tight conical habit and glossy green foliage. **Withstands trimming**. Also makes a fine specimen tree.

Thuja plicata 'Fastigiata'

A fast growing, narrow conifer which makes an excellent specimen plant, and is good for hedging, where only a minimum of clipping is necessary. The foliage is bright green and pleasantly fragrant when crushed.

Thuja plicata 'Rogersii'

A fine dwarf conifer which forms a rounded bush, occasionally sending up leader shoots which make it conical. The foliage is golden bronze making this plant very valuable for the conifer and heather garden.

Thuja plicata 'Zebrina'

A very attractive, medium growing conifer with foliage light green, striped greeny yellow, particularly bright in summer. Excellent specimen plant and can be used for screening.

Thujopsis dolobrata

This unusual conifer forms a rounded bush in its early days and is conical with age. The branchlets are flattened, and the foliage is shining green above with a conspicuous, silver white band below.

Tsuga canadensis 'Jeddeloh'

A semi prostrate conifer, with very graceful, light green foliage adding something quite different in form and texture to our range for the rockery, conifer and heather garden.

Tsuga heterophylla

A tree more than 200 ft. high in its native forests of western North America, and much used for timber production. Introduced into Scotland in 1852. It makes an elegant specimen tree with wide spreading branches. The cones are stalkless and rich purple when young. **Growth is rapid when suited, 2 to 3 ft. a year**. Not suitable for small gardens except as a hedge.

Ulex europaeus 'Plenus'

A superb shrub when, in April and May it is smothered in long lasting, semi double yellow flowers.

Vaccinium corymbosum

Makes a most attractive garden shrub with racemes of pinkish white flowers in May, which remain on the bush for some time before the edible blue fruits form. It also has very good autumn tinted foliage.

Vaccinium corymbosum 'Blue Ray'

An erect growing, vigorous bush, which produces long stems of tightly clustered berries, which are very large, firm and pale blue with a fairly small scar. **Good flavour**. This variety is inclined to produce many young stems and these should be thinned out. Ripening July to mid-August and an excellent cropper, particularly when pollinated by another variety.

Vaccinium corymbosum 'Grover'

A vigorous growing bush which produces clusters of dark-blue, very large fruits, ripening in mid season, September. A good cropper, which produces well on its own pollen but is even better when pollinated by another variety. As a bonus the Blueberries have **excellent autumn leaf colour**.

Vestia foetida

A small, erect growing evergreen with nodding, tubular flowers of pale yellow from April to July.

Viburnum carlesii 'Aurora'

An improved form of 'Carlesii'. Red buds open to pink fragrant flowers in April and May. In autumn the leaves have rich colours.

Viburnum davidii

A small evergreen making good ground cover. Flowers are white on flat heads. They are followed by turquoise blue berries when groups of plants are planted close together.

Viburnum opulus

A vigorous shrub with maple like leaves which colour richly in autumn. White, flattened heads of flowers in May and June are followed by glistening red bunches of berries.

Viburnum opulus 'Fructuluteo'

A vigorous shrub with flat heads of fertile flowers in June or July, that look similar to a lacecap Hydrangea. They are followed by yellow berries and rich autumn foliage tints.

Viburnum opulus 'Nanum'

A curious dwarf form, with dense tufted habit, occasionally producing flat, white heads of flowers and red berries. **Excellent autumn colours**.

Viburnum opulus 'Sterile'

A popular hardy shrub with round white flower heads like snowballs in May and June. **Very easy to please**.

Viburnum opulus 'Xanthocarpum'

A broad compact bush with white lace-cap flowers followed by translucent amber-yellow berries in the autumn which persist after leaf fall.

Viburnum plicatum 'Lanarth'

A very fine form with upright, tiered growth. The wide flat flower heads consist of fertile flowers surrounded by white, sterile florets. The foliage has attractive autumn colour.

Viburnum plicatum 'Mariesii'

A superb shrub, the abundance of white flowers in May and June gives the effect of a snow laden bush. Excellent autumn colours.

Viburnum plicatum 'Pink Beauty'

A superb selection from Viburnum plic. tomentosum, where the ray florets turn to pink as they age. The growth is wide spreading with tiered branches and the umbels of the flower resemble a lace cap hydranga. In a good Autumn the leaves colour long before falling.

Viburnum plicatum 'Watanabei'

A form of V. plicatum with a very dense habit and a long flowering season, with its main display in June when established. Although termed 'nanum' it can reach a height of 6 feet, but can be kept dwarf with pruning, which can delay flowering. A lovely flowering shrub for the smaller garden. The original plant was found growing wild in Japan.

Viburnum plicatum tomentosum

A large, wide spreading shrub with branches growing in layers, creating in time, an attractive and characteristic tiered effect. Creamy white flowers in May and June are followed by red fruit that finally turns black.

Viburnum rhytidophyllum

A fast growing evergreen with large, attractively corrugated leaves, dark glossy green above, dense grey hairs beneath. Creamy white flowers appear in May followed by red fruits that turn black.

Viburnum tinus

A very easy and popular evergreen, flowers pink in bud, opening to white from September to April, followed by dark blue fruits. **Can be used as informal screen**.

Viburnum tinus 'Eve Price'

One of our favourite shrubs, valuable winter colour, long flowering. Pink buds open white from September to March, followed by dark blue berries. Evergreen with very compact habit. **Can be used as screening**.

Viburnum tinus 'Gwenllian'

A valuable winter flowering evergreen with rich pink buds opening to long lasting, blushing white flowers. Dark blue berries follow. **Can be used for hedging and screening**.

Viburnum x bodnantense 'Dawn'

A gem of a shrub to brighten up the garden in winter. Richly scented, rose pink flowers appear from autumn into winter.

Viburnum x burkwoodii

An outstanding evergreen with clusters of fragrant, pink budded, white flowers in April and May.

Viburnum x carlcephalum

A splendid compact shrub producing broad, rounded heads 5'-6' across, of pink budded, white, fragrant flowers in May. Excellent autumn colours.

Viburnum x juddii

A delightful shrub of compact habit, producing clusters of sweetly scented, pink tinted flowers in April and May.

Vinca major

A vigorous evergreen shrub producing blue flowers from April to June. **Ideal for covering banks and waste areas**.

Vinca major 'Variegata' (Elegantissima)

A vigorous evergreen sub shrub with handsome foliage coloured green and cream. Pale blue periwinkle flowers appear from April to June.

Vinca minor

A ground cover evergreen that will grow in dense shade and make a carpet of green. Blue flowers appear from April to June and sporadically until autumn.

Vinca minor 'Atropurpurea'

A very attractive form of periwinkle with deep, plum purple flowers appearing from March to July, often intermittently until October. **Useful evergreen ground cover for a shady spot**.

Vinca minor 'Bowles' Variety'

A very easy to please ground cover evergreen with blue flowers. **Ideal for deep shade** in areas where many plants will not grow easily, spreading and making a low carpet of green.

Weigela 'Abel Carriere'

A free flowering shrub with bright rose carmine flowers, flecked gold in the throat. Best pruned after flowering by shortening or removal of flowering stems.

Weigela 'Bristol Ruby'

A vigorous, erect growing shrub with ruby red flowers in May and June. Best pruned after flowering by shortening or removal of flowering stems.

Weigela 'Newport Red' (Vanicek)

A superb weigela, vigorous and upright growing. Light red flowers appear in May and June, often again in early autumn. Pruning should consist of the shortening or removal of flowering stems.

Weigela florida 'Foliis Purpureis'

An attractive, dwarf variety of Weigela. Compact habit, purple flushed leaves and pink flowers in May and June.

Weigela florida 'Variegata'

A fine variegated shrub. Gold and green foliage with pink bell flowers in May and June. Prune after flowering to keep good shape.

Yucca filamentosa

An outstanding evergreen with strap like leaves edged with curly white threads. Creamy white flowers appear on erect, conical stems 3'-6' high in July and August.

Yucca gloriosa 'Variegata'

A slow growing evergreen with strap like leaves, striped and margined yellow. Not a regular flowerer but the flowers are creamy white bells in conical panicles. Treat as a foliage plant - the flower is a bonus.

SHRUBS, CONIFERS, HEATHERS

BOTANICAL NAME	COMMON NAME
Abies koreana	– Korean Fir
Abies lasiocarpa 'Compacta'	– Alpine Fir
Acer griseum	– Paperbark Maple
Acer japonicum 'Aconitifolium' (Laciniatum)	– Japanese Maple
Acer palmatum	– Japanese Maple
Agave americana 'Mediopicta'	– Century Plant
Amelanchier canadensis (Lamarckii)	– June Berry
Andromeda polifolia 'Compacta'	– Bog Rosemary
Aralia elata	– Chinese Angelica Tree
Araucaria araucana	– Monkey Puzzle
Arbutus unedo	– Killarney Strawberry Tree
Aronia arbutifolia	– Red Chokeberry
Artemesia absinthium 'Lambrook silver'	– Wormwood or Absinth
Arundinaria	– Bamboo
Arundinaria pygmaea	– Bamboo, Dwarf
Aucuba japonica	– Spotted Laurel
Azalea japonica	– Japanese Azalea
Berberis	– Barberry
Buddleia davidii	– Butterfly Bush
Buddleia globosa	– Chilean Orange Ball Tree
Buxus sempervirens	– Box
Buxus sempervirens 'Elegantissima'	– Variegated Box
Callistemon linearis	– Australian Bottle Brush
Calluna vulgaris	– Ling Heather
Caryopteris x clandonensis	– Blue Spiraea
Catalpa bignonioides 'Aurea'	– Golden Indian Bean Tree
Ceanothus	– Californian Lilac
Ceanothus thyrsiflorus	– Creeping Blue Blossom
Cedrus atlantica 'Glauca'	– Blue Cedar
Cedrus deodara	– Deodar
Cedrus deodara 'Aurea'	– Golden Deodar
Cedrus deodara 'Golden Horizon'	– Golden Deodar
Cedrus libani	– Cedar of Lebanon
Cephalanthus occidentalis	– The Button Bush
Ceratostigma plumbaginoides	– Hardy Plumbago
Cercis siliquastrum	– Judas Tree
Chaenomeles	– Japonica, Flowering Quince.
Chamaecyparis lawsoniana	– Lawson Cypress
Chimonanthus praecox	– Winter Sweet
Choisya ternata	– Mexican Orange Blossom
Cistus	– Sun Rose, Rock Rose
Colutea arborescens 'Copper Beauty'	– Bladder Senna
Cordyline australis	– New Zealand Cabbage Tree
Cornus	– Red Barked Dogwood
Cornus canadensis	– Creeping Dogwood
Cornus mas	– Cornelian Cherry
Cortaderia	– Pampas Grass

BOTANICAL NAME	COMMON NAME
Cortaderia selloana 'Rosea'	– Pink Pampas
Corylus avellana	– Hazel
Corylus avellana 'Contorta'	– Corkscrew Hazel
Corylus maxima 'Purpurea'	– Purple Filbert Nut
Cotinus coggygria	– Smoke Tree
Crataegus monogyna	– Quick Thorn
Cryptomeria japonica	– Japanese Cedar
Cupressocyparis leylandii 'Castlewellan'	– Golden Leyland
Cupressus macrocarpa 'Goldcrest'	– Monterey Cypress
Cytisus	– Broom
Daboecia cantabrica	– St Dabeoc's Heath
Daphne cneorum	– Garland Flower
Daphne mezereum	– Mezereon
Embothrium coccineum 'Longifolium'	– Chilean Fire Bush
Erica arborea	– Tree Heather
Erica carnea	– Winter Flowering Heather
Erica cinerea	– Bell Heath or Heather
Erica erigena	– Irish or Spring Heath
Erica lusitanica	– Tree Heather
Erica tetralix	– Cross Leaved Heath
Erica vagans	– Cornish Heath
Erica x darleyensis	– Winter Flowering Hybrid
Eucalyptus gunnii	– Gum Tree
Fagus sylvatica	– Beech
Fagus sylvatica 'Purpurea'	– Copper Beech, Purple Beech
Fatsia japonica (Aralia sieboldii)	– False Caster Oil Plant
Fremontodendron 'California Glory'	– California Glory Bush
Gaultheria procumbens	– Checkerberry, Partridge Berry
Genista aetnesis	– Mount Etna Broom
Genista hispanica	– Spanish Gorse
Genista tinctoria	– Dyer's Greenweed
Ginkgo biloba	– Maidenhair Tree
Hamamelis mollis	– Chinese Witch Hazel
Hedera canariensis 'Variegata'	– Gloire de Marengo, Canary Island Ivy
Hedera colchica 'Dentata Variegata'	– Variegated Persian Ivy
Hedera	– Ivy
Hydrangea 'Blue Wave'	– Lacecap Hydrangea
Hypericum calycinum	– Rose of Sharon
Ilex	– Holly
Jasminum nudiflorum	– Winter Jasmine
Juniperus	– Juniper
Juniperus chinensis 'Aurea'	– Young's Golden Juniper
Juniperus communis 'Hibernica'	– Irish Juniper
Juniperus conferta	– Shore Juniper
Kalmia angustifolia 'Rubra'	– Sheep Laurel
Kalmia latifolia	– Calico Bush
Kerria japonica	– Jew's Mallow

BOTANICAL NAME	COMMON NAME
Kerria japonica 'Pleniflora'	– Bachelor's Button
Kolkwitzia amabilis	– Beauty Bush
Larix decidua	– Larch
Larix kaempferi 'Pendula'	– Japanese Larch
Lavandula	– Lavender
Lavandula 'Vera'	– Dutch Lavender
Lavatera olbia	– Mallow
Ligustrum japonicum 'Rotundifolium'	– Japanese Privet
Ligustrum ovalifolium	– Privet
Ligustrum ovalifolium 'Argenteum'	– Silver Privet
Ligustrum ovalifolium 'Aureum'	– Golden Privet
Mahonia aquifolium	– Oregon Grape
Malus	– Crab Apple
Malus floribunda	– Japanese Crab
Metasequoia glyptostroboides	– Dawn Redwood
Nandina domestica	– Chinese Sacred Bamboo
Olearia haastii	– Daisy Bush
Olearia macrodonta	– New Zealand Holly
Paeonia suffruticosa (arborea)	– Tree Paeony, Moutan Paeony
Philadelphus	– Mock Orange
Phlomis fruticosa	– Jerusalem Sage
Phormium tenax	– New Zealand Flax
Phygelius capensis	– Cape Figwort
Picea abies	– Christmas Tree, Norway Spruce
Picea	– Spruce
Picea brewerana	– Brewer Weeping Spruce
Picea glauca 'Alberta Globe'	– White Spruce
Picea glauca 'Albertiana Conica'	– Alberta White Spruce
Picea mariana	– Black Spruce
Picea omorika	– Serbian Spruce
Picea orientalis 'Aurea"('Aureospicata')	– Oriental Spruce
Picea pungens	– Blue Spruce
Pinus aristata	– Bristlecone Pine
Pinus mugo	– Mountain Pine
Pinus nigra	– Austrian Pine
Pinus parviflora	– Japanese White Pine
Pinus strobus 'Nana' _Dwf white_	– Pine
Pinus sylvestris	– Scots Pine
Pinus wallichiana ('Griffithii')	– Bhutan Pine
Prunus 'Cistena'	– Purple Leaf Sand Cherry
Prunus 'Kanzan'	– Japanese Cherry
Prunus cerasifera 'Nigra'	– Flowering Plum
Prunus cerasifera 'Pissardii'	– Purple Leaf Plum
Prunus laurocerasus	– Laurel
Prunus lusitanica	– Portugal Laurel
Prunus serrulata 'Amanogawa'	– The Poplar Cherry
Prunus subhirtella 'Autumnalis Rosea'	– Winter Cherry

BOTANICAL NAME	COMMON NAME
Prunus tenella	– Dwarf Russian Almond
Punica granatum 'Nana'	– Dwarf pomegranate
Pyracantha	– Firethorn
Rhododendron kiusianum	– Kyushu Azalea
Rhus typhina	– Stag's Horn Sumach
Ribes sanguineum	– Flowering Currant
Robinia hispida 'Rosea'	– Rose Acacia
Romneya coulteri	– Tree Poppy
Romneya x hybrida	– Californian Poppy
Rosmarinus officinalis	– Rosemary
Rubus tricolor	– Ornamental Blackberry
Ruta graveolens 'Jackman's Blue'	– Rue
Salix hastata 'Wehrhahnii'	– Dwarf Willow
Salix lanata	– Woolly Willow
Salix sachalinensis 'Sekka'	– Willow
Salvia officinalis 'Purpurascens'	– Purple Leaf Sage
Sambucus racemosa 'Plumosa Aurea'	– Golden Elder
Santolina chamaecyparissus	– Cotton Lavender
Sarcococca	– Christmas Box
Sophora japonica	– Japanese Pagoda Tree
Spartium junceum	– Spanish Broom
Spiraea x arguta	– Bridal Wreath
Symphoricarpos albus	– Snowberry
Syringa microphylla 'Superba'	– Dwarf Lilac
Syringa	– Lilac
Syringa velutina (syn. palibiniana)	– Korean Lilac
Tamarix	– Tamarisk
Taxus baccata	– Common Yew
Taxus baccata 'Fastigiata Aurea'	– Golden Irish Yew
Taxus baccata 'Fastigiata'	– Irish Yew
Taxus baccata 'Semperaurea'	– Golden Yew
Teucrium fruticans	– Shrubby Germander
Thuja orientalis 'Elegantissma'	– Chinese Arbor-vitae
Thuja plicata	– Western Red Cedar
Tsuga canadensis 'Jeddeloh'	– Eastern Hemlock
Tsuga heterophylla	– Western Hemlock
Ulex europaeus 'Plenus'	– Gorse
Vaccinium corymbosum	– Blueberry
Viburnum opulus	– Guelder Rose
Viburnum opulus 'Sterile'	– Snowball Tree
Viburnum tinus	– Laurustinus
Vinca major	– Greater Periwinkle
Vinca minor	– Lesser Periwinkle
Yucca gloriosa 'Variegata'	– Adam's Needle

SHRUBS, CONIFERS, HEATHERS

COMMON NAME	BOTANICAL NAME
Absinth	– Artemesia absinthium
Adam's Needle	– Yucca
Alberta White Spruce	– Picea glauca 'Albertiana Conica'
Alpine Fir	– Abies lasiocarpa
Alpine or Winter Heath	– Erica carnea
Bottle Brush	– Callistemon
Austrian Pine	– Pinus nigra
Azalea	– Rhododendron (see under Azalea)
Bachelor's Button	– Kerria japonica
Bamboo	– Arundinaria
Barberry	– Berberis
Beauty Bush	– Kolkwitzia amabilis
Beech	– Fagus sylvatica
Bell Heath	– Erica cinerea
Black Spruce	– Picea mariana
Bladder Senna	– Colutea arborescens 'Copper Beauty'
Blue Cedar	– Cedrus atlantica 'Glauca'
Blue Spiraea	– Caryopteris
Blue Spruce	– Picea pungens
Bog Rosemary	– Andromeda
Box	– Buxus
Brewer Weeping Spruce	– Picea brewerana
Bridal Wreath	– Spiraea x arguta
Bristlecone Pine	– Pinus aristata
Broom	– Cytisus & Genista & Spartium
Butterfly Bush	– Buddleia davidii
Calico Bush	– Kalmia latifolia
California Glory Bush	– Fremontodendron 'California Glory'
Californian Lilac	– Ceanothus
Californian Poppy	– Romneya
Cape Figwort	– Phygelius
Cedar of Lebanon	– Cedrus libani
Century Plant	– Agave
Checkerberry, Partridge Berry	– Gaultheria procumbens
Cherry	– Prunus
Chilean Fire Bush	– Embothrium coccineum
Chilean Orange Ball Tree	– Buddleia globosa
Chinese Angelica Tree	– Aralia elata
Chinese Arbor-vitae	– Thuja orientalis 'Elegantissma'
Chinese Sacred Bamboo	– Nandina domestica
Chinese Witch Hazel	– Hamamelis mollis
Christmas Box	– Sarcococca
Christmas Tree, Norway Spruce	– Picea abies
Common Yew	– Taxus baccata
Copper Beech, Purple Beech	– Fagus sylvatica 'Purpurea'
Coral Bark Maple	– Acer palmatum 'Senkaki'
Corkscrew Hazel	– Corylus avellana 'Contorta'

157

COMMON NAME	BOTANICAL NAME
Cornelian Cherry	– Cornus mas
Cornish Heath	– Erica vagans
Cotton Lavender	– Santolina chamaecyparissus
Crab Apple	– Malus
Creeping Blue Blossom	– Ceanothus thyrsiflorus repens 'Gnome'
Creeping Dogwood	– Cornus canadensis
Cross Leaved Heath	– Erica tetralix
Cypress	– Cupressus
Daisy Bush	– Olearia haastii
Dawn Redwood	– Metasequoia glyptostroboides
Deciduous Azalea	– Rhododendron(see Azalea)
Deodar	– Cedrus deodara
Dogwood	– Cornus
Dutch Lavender	– Lavandula 'Vera'
Dwarf Lilac	– Syringa microphylla
Dwarf Russian Almond	– Prunus tenella
Dwarf pomegranate	– Punica granatum 'Nana'
Dyer's Greenweed	– Genista tinctoria
Eastern Hemlock	– Tsuga canadensis
Elder	– Sambuca
Evergreen Azalea	– Azalea japonica Rhododendron
False Caster Oil Plant	– Fatsia japonica
False Cypress	– Chamaecyparis
Firethorn	– Pyracantha
Filbert	– Corylus
Flowering Currant	– Ribes sanquineum
Flowering Dogwood	– Cornus florida
Flowering Dogwood	– Cornus florida 'Rainbow'
Flowering Plum	– Prunus cerasifera 'Nigra'
Garland Flower	– Daphne cneorum
Gorse	– Ulex europaeus
Greater Periwinkle	– Vinca major
Guelder Rose	– Viburnum opulus
Gum Tree	– Eucalypyus
Hardy Plumbago	– Ceratostigma
Hazel	– Corylus avellana
Heather	– Calluna Erica
Hemlock	– Tsuga
Holly	– Ilex
Irish Juniper	– Juniperus communis 'Hibernica'
Irish Yew	– Taxus baccata 'Fastigiata'
Irish Heath	– Erica erigena
Ivy	– Hedera
Japanese Azalea	– Azalea japonica (Rhododendron)
Japanese Cedar	– Cryptomeria japonica
Japanese Cherry	– Prunus
Japanese Crab	– Malus floribunda
Japanese Larch	– Larix kaempferi
Japanese Maple	– Acer palmatum

COMMON NAME	BOTANICAL NAME
Japanese Pagoda Tree	– Sophora japonica
Japanese Privet	– Ligustrum japonicum
Japanese White Pine	– Pinus parviflora
Japonica, Flowering Quince	– Chaenomeles
Jerusalem Sage	– Phlomis fruticosa
Jew's Mallow	– Kerria japonica
Judas Tree	– Cercis siliquastrum
June Berry	– Amelanchier canadensis (Lamarckii)
Juniper	– Juniperus
Killarney Strawberry Tree	– Arbutus unedo
Korean Fir	– Abies koreana
Korean Lilac	– Syringa velutina (syn. palibiniana)
Kyushu Azalea	– Rhododendron kiusianum
Lace Cap Hydrandea	– Hydrangea serrata 'Preziosa'
Lacecap Hydrangea	– Hydrangea 'Blue Wave'
Larch	– Larix decidua
Laurel	– Prunus laurocerasus
Laurustinus	– Viburnum tinus
Lavender	– Lavandula
Lawson Cypress	– Chamaecyparis lawsoniana
Lilac	– Syringa
Ling	– Calluna vulgaris
Mallow	– Lavatera olbia
Mexican Orange Blossom	– Choisya ternata
Mezereon	– Daphne mezereum
Mock Orange	– Philadelphus
Monkey Puzzle	– Araucaria araucana
Monterey Cypress	– Cupressus macrocarpa
Mop Head Hydrangea	– Hydrangea hortensis
Mount Etna Broom	– Genista aetnesis
Mountain Pine	– Pinus mugo
Myrtle	– Myrtus
New Zealand Cabbage Tree	– Cordyline australis
New Zealand Flax	– Phormium tenax
New Zealand Holly	– Olearia macrodonta
Norway Spruce	– Picea abies
Nut	– Corylus
Oregon Grape	– Mahonia aquifolium
Oriental Spruce	– Picea orientalis
Ornamental Blackberry	– Rubus tricolor
Pampas Grass	– Cortaderia
Paperbark Maple	– Acer griseum
Partridge Berry	– Gaultheria procumbens
Periwinkle	– Vinca
Persian Ivy	– Hedera colchica
Pfitzer Juniper	– Juniperus x media 'Pfitzerana'
Pine	– Pinus
Pink Pampas	– Cortaderia selloana 'Rosea'
Plum	– Prunus

COMMON NAME	BOTANICAL NAME
Portugal Laurel	– Prunus lusitanica
Privet	– Ligustrum ovalifolium
Purple Filbert Nut	– Corylus maxima 'Purpurea'
Purple Leaf Plum	– Prunus cerasifera 'Pissardii'
Quick Thorn	– Crataegus monogyna
Red Barked Dogwood	– Cornus alba 'Elegantissima'
Rock Rose	– Cistus
Red Chokeberry	– Aronia arbutifolia
Rose Acacia	– Robinia hispida 'Rosea'
Rose of Sharon	– Hypericum calycinum
Rosemary	– Rosmarinus officinalis
Rue	– Ruta graveolens
Sacred Bamboo	– Nandina domestica
Scots Pine	– Pinus sylvestris 'Watereri'
Serbian Spruce	– Picea omorika
Sheep Laurel	– Kalmia augustifolia
Shore Juniper	– Juniperus conferta
Shrubby Germander	– Teucrium fruticans
Smoke Tree	– Cotinus coggygria
Snowball Tree	– Viburnum opulus 'Sterile'
Snowberry	– Symphoricarpos albus
Spanish Broom	– Spartium junceum
Spanish Gorse	– Genista hispanica
Spotted Laural	– Aucuba japonica 'Picturata'
Spotted Laurel	– Aucuba japonica
Spruce	– Picea
St Dabeoc's Heath	– Daboecia
Stag's Horn Sumach	– Rhus typhina
Standard Lilac	– Syringa microphylla 'Superba' (Standard)
Sun Rose	– Cistus
Tamarisk	– Tamarix
Tree Heather	– Erica lusitanica
Tree Heather	– Erica arborea
Tree Paeony, Moutan Paeony	– Paeonia suffruticosa (arborea)
Veronica	– Hebe
Warminster Broom	– Cytisus x praecox
Western Hemlock	– Tsuga heterophylla
Western Red Cedar	– Thuja plicata
Westonbirt Dogwood	– Cornus alba 'Sibirica' ("Westonbirt')
White Spruce	– Picea glauca
Willow	– Salix
Winter Cherry	– Prunus subhirtella 'Autumnalis Rosea'
Winter Flowering Heather	– Erica carnea
Winter Flowering Hybrid,Heather	– Erica x darleynsis
Winter Jasmine	– Jasminum nudiflorum
Winter Sweet	– Chimonanthus praecox
Witch Hazel	– Hamamelis x intermedia 'Diane'
Witch Hazel	– Hamamelis

COMMON NAME	BOTANICAL NAME
Woolly Willow	– Salix lanata
Wormwood or Absinth	– Artemesia absinthium
Yew	– Taxus
Young's Golden Juniper	– Juniperus chinensis 'Aurea'

Climbers up to a
Height of Twelve Foot

Height up to 12 ft.

		TYPE	DECIDUOUS/EVERGREEN	MOISTURE LEVEL	LIGHT	SOIL	POSITION	BEST MONTH
Campsis grandiflora		S	D	N	F	N	S	8-9
Clematis Barbara Jackman		S	D	N	A	C	A	5-6
	Comtesse de Bouchaud	S	D	N	A	C	A	6-9
	Duchess of Edinburgh	S	D	N	A	C	A	5-6
	Elsa Spath (Xerxes)	S	D	N	FP	C	A	6-9
	Hagley Hybrid	S	D	N	A	C	A	6-9
	Lasurstern	S	D	N	FP	C	A	5-6
	Miss Bateman	S	D	N	A	C	A	5-6
	Mrs Cholmondeley	S	D	N	A	C	A	5-9
	Mrs N.Thompson	S	D	N	A	C	A	5-6
	Nelly Moser	S	D	N	S	C	A	5-6
	Rouge Cardinal	S	D	N	FP	C	A	6-9
	Sealand Gem	S	D	N	A	C	A	6-9
	The President	S	D	N	A	C	A	6-9
	Ville de Lyon	S	D	N	FP	C	A	7-10
	Voluceau	S	D	N	FP	C	A	6-9
	Vyvyan Pennell	S	D	N	FP	C	A	5-6
Clematis alpina		S	D	N	S	C	A	4-5
Clematis macropetala		S	D	N	A	C	A	4-5
Clematis macropetala	Markham's Pink	S	D	N	A	C	A	4-5
Clematis x durandii		S	D	N	FP	C	A	6-9
Eccremocarpus scaber		S	D	N	FP	N	S	6-8
Hedera canariensis	Variegata	S	E	A	A	N	A	1-12
Hedera colchica	Dentata Variegata	S	E	A	A	N	A	1-12

Height up to 12 ft.

		BEST MONTH	POSITION	SOIL	LIGHT	MOISTURE LEVEL	DECIDUOUS/EVERGREEN	TYPE
Hedera colchica	Paddy's Pride (Sulphur Heart)	S	E	A	A	N	A	1-12
Hedera helix	Anna Marie	S	E	A	A	N	A	1-12
	Boskoop	S	E	A	A	N	A	1-12
	Cavendishii	S	E	A	A	N	A	1-12
	Cristata	S	E	A	A	N	A	1-12
	Gavotte	S	E	A	A	N	A	1-12
	Glacier	S	E	A	A	N	A	1-12
	Goldheart	S	E	A	A	N	A	1-12
	Green Ripple	S	E	A	A	N	A	1-12
	Ivalace	S	E	A	A	N	A	1-12
	Little Picture	S	E	A	A	N	A	1-12
	Lutzii	S	E	A	A	N	A	1-12
Hydrangea petiolaris		S	D	A	A	N	A	6-7
Lonicera	Dropmore Scarlet	S	D	A	FP	N	A	7-8
Lonicera henryi		S	E	A	FP	N	A	6-7
Lonicera x heckrottii	Gold Flame	S	D	A	FP	N	A	7-9
Lonicera x tellmanniana		S	D	A	S	N	A	6-7
Schizophragma hydrangeoides		S	D	N	A	N	A	7-8
Solanum crispum	Glasnevin	S	E	N	F	C	S	6-9
Trachelospermum jasminoides		S	E	N	F	N	S	7-8
Actinidia chinensis		S	D	N	F	N	S	6-8
Actinidia kolomikta		S	D	N	F	N	S	6-9

Climbers above a
Height of Twelve Foot

Height above 12 ft.

		BEST MONTH	POSITION	SOIL	LIGHT	MOISTURE LEVEL	DECIDUOUS/EVERGREEN	TYPE
Ampelopsis brevipedunculata	Elegans	S	D	N	F	N	S	1-12
Campsis radicans		S	D	N	F	N	S	8-9
Campsis radicans	Yellow Trumpet	S	D	N	F	N	S	8-9
Campsis x tagliabuana	Madame Galen	S	D	N	F	N	S	8-9
Celastrus scandens		S	D	W	A	N	A	9-10
Clematis	Gipsy Queen	S	D	N	FP	C	A	8-10
	Huldine	S	D	N	FP	C	A	7-10
	Jackmanii Alba	S	D	N	A	C	A	6-9
	Jackmanii Superba	S	D	N	A	C	A	6-9
	Jackmanii	S	D	N	A	C	A	6-9
	Lady Betty Balfour	S	D	N	F	C	A	9-10
	Lawsoniana	S	D	N	FP	C	A	6-9
	Madame Baron Veillard	S	D	N	F	C	A	9-10
	Ramona (syn. hybrida Sieboldii)	S	D	N	A	C	A	6-9
	William Kennett	S	D	N	A	C	A	6-9
Clematis armandii		S	E	N	FP	C	S	3-4
Clematis flammula		S	D	N	FP	C	A	8-10
Clematis montana		S	D	N	A	C	A	5
Clematis montana	Elizabeth	S	D	N	A	C	A	5-6
Clematis montana	Grandiflora	S	D	N	A	C	A	5-6
Clematis montana	Tetrarose	S	D	N	A	C	A	5-6
Clematis montana rubens		S	D	N	A	C	A	5-6
Clematis montana wilsonii		S	D	N	A	C	A	6-7

Height above 12 ft.

	BEST MONTH	POSITION	SOIL	LIGHT	MOISTURE LEVEL	DECIDUOUS/EVERGREEN	TYPE
Clematis spooneri		S	D	N	A	C	A	5-6
Clematis tangutica		S	D	N	FP	C	A	7-10
Clematis Marie Boisselot (syn. Madame le Coultre)		S	D	N	A	C	A	6-9
Hedera Helix Hibernica		S	E	A	A	N	A	1-12
Jasminum officinale		S	D	A	FP	N	A	6-9
Lonicera (general)		S	E	A	FP	N	A	6-9
Lonicera japonica Aureo-reticulata		S	E	A	FP	N	A	5-6
Halliana		S	E	A	FP	N	A	6-10
Lonicera japonica var.repens (L.Flexuosa)		S	E	A	FP	N	A	6-10
Lonicera periclymenum Belgica		S	D	A	FP	N	A	5-6
Serotina		S	D	A	FP	N	A	7-9
Lonicera x americana		S	D	A	FP	N	A	6-7
Parthenocissus henryana		S	D	A	A	N	A	6-10
Parthenocissus quinquefolia		S	D	A	A	N	A	9-10
Parthenocissus tricuspidata Veitchii		S	D	A	A	N	A	9-10
Passiflora caerulea		S	D	N	FP	N	S	6-9
Pileostegia viburnoides		S	E	N	A	N	A	8-10
Polygonum baldschuanicum		S	D	A	A	N	E	7-9
Solanum jasminoides Album		S	E	N	FP	N	S	7-10
Vitis Brant (vinifera Brandt)		S	D	A	FP	C	E	9-10
Vitis coignetiae		S	D	A	A	C	E	9-10
Wisteria floribunda Macrobotrys		S	D	A	F	A	A	5
Peaches and Cream		S	D	A	F	A	A	5-6

Height above 12 ft.

		BEST MONTH	POSITION	SOIL	LIGHT	MOISTURE LEVEL	DECIDUOUS/EVERGREEN	TYPE
Wisteria floribunda	Purple Patches	S	D	A	F	A	A	5-6
	Rosea	S	D	A	F	A	A	5-6
Wisteria sinensis		S	D	A	F	A	A	5-6
Wisteria sinensis	Pink Ice (Honbeni)	S	D	A	F	A	A	5-6
	Reindeer (Jakoh Fuji)	S	D	A	F	A	A	5-6

PLANT DESCRIPTIONS
CLIMBERS

Actinidia chinensis

A vigorous ornamental climber with large, heart shaped leaves and reddish, hairy shoots and stems. Clusters of fragrant, creamy white flowers, maturing to buff yellow, appear from June to August. They are followed by edible, gooseberry flavoured fruits. May need initial support.

Actinidia kolomikta

A striking, slender climber with eye catching foliage. Each dark green, heart shaped leaf is marked with pink or white at the end, every one different. Slightly fragrant, white flowers appear in June, sometimes followed by sweet tasting fruits. Best colour obtained on a south or west facing wall in full sun. May need initial support.

Ampelopsis brevipedunculata 'Elegans'

A very lovely and vigorous climber introduced before 1850 by Siebold. The leaves are 3 or 5 lobed and handsomly splashed with pink and white, and the young shoots are pink. It is not reliably hardy and must have the protection of a south or south-west wall. An ideal climber for an unheated conservatory.

Campsis grandiflora

A beautiful, oriental climber with large, deep orange and red, trumpet shaped flowers in drooping clusters during August and Sept. Needs a sheltered spot and support till the aerial roots appear. Protect plant base in winter until well established.

Campsis radicans

A hardy climbing plant with superb scarlet and orange, trumpet shaped flowers appearing in August and September. The plant climbs by aerial roots but needs some support till established. Also protect the roots with bracken or dry peat from early winter to spring for the first few years.

Campsis radicans 'Yellow Trumpet'

A hardy climbing plant, the yellow form of Campsis radicans gained an Award of Merit in 1969. Large golden yellow trumpet flowers in late summer. Self supporting when established. Protect roots in winter.

Campsis x tagliabuana 'Madame Galen'

A hardy climbing plant with clusters of salmon red, trumpet shaped flowers in August and September. Protect during the first few winters by covering with dry peat or bracken, removing in spring.

Celastrus scandens

A vigorous climbing shrub. Female plants produce orange capsules. Ideal to grow through unsightly hedges and trees. If grown against a wall, needs support eg. trellis etc.

Clematis 'Barbara Jackman'

A large flowered hybrid with single, soft petunia mauve flowers with crimson bars in May, June and Sept. Suitable for any aspect. When planted in sun it is best to shade the roots. No regular pruning needed.

Clematis 'Comtesse de Bouchaud'

A very free flowering and vigorous variety producing slightly smaller flowers than the average hybrid, but many more, and continuously from June to September. The flowers are a mauve/pink colour.

Clematis 'Duchess of Edinburgh'

A double white flowered clematis of moderate vigor, growing to 8-12ft. The slightly scented flowers 4'-6' across are rosette shaped, white with a tinge of green and with yellow stamens, borne in May,June and September, when the flowers on the new growth will be single. Suitable for any aspect. A cool root run is essential.

Clematis 'Elsa Spath' (Xerxes)

Large flowers,6-8 ins diam., deep violet blue with purple shading,dark stamens of reddish purple. A beautifully shaped flower with a long flowering season. Does not require regular pruning. Suitable for any aspect except North facing.

Clematis 'Gipsy Queen'

A vigorous, single flowered hybrid with large, rich violet purple flowers with a velvet sheen and reddish purple stamens. Very free flowering from August to Oct. Suitable for East, South or West aspect. Best position has roots in shade, top in sun.

Clematis 'Hagley Hybrid'

A single flowered hybrid with large, shell pink flowers, brown stamens and pointed sepals. Very free flowering from June to Sept. Suitable for any aspect. When planted in sun it is best to shade the roots. No regular pruning needed.

Clematis 'Huldine'

A vigorous, free flowering hybrid, with pearly white, single flowers with a pale mauve bar on the reverse of each petal, appearing from July to October. Suitable for East, South or West facing aspect. Best position has roots in shade, top in sun.

Clematis 'Jackmanii'

A popular hybrid, vigorous and free flowering with single purple flowers and greenish stamens, produced from July to Oct. Suitable for East, South or West facing aspect. Best position has roots in shade, top in sun.

Clematis 'Jackmanii Alba'

The white form of 'Jackmanii', vigorous and free flowering from June to September,will sometimes produce semi double, bluish white flowers in early summer. Suitable for any aspect. When planted in sun it is best to shade the roots.

Clematis 'Jackmanii Superba'

A large flowered hybrid with single, deep velvet purple flowers with green stamens. Broader petals than 'Jackmanii'. Suitable for any aspect. When planted in sun it is best to shade the roots.

Clematis 'Lady Betty Balfour'

A vigorous, free flowering variety with large, violet blue flowers and yellow stamens, appearing in September and October. Needs full sun.

Clematis 'Lasurstern'

A very handsome and showy variety, producing rich lavender blue flowers with cream stamens in May, June and Sept. Suitable for East, South or West aspect. Best position has roots in shade, top in sun. No pruning needed.

Clematis 'Lawsoniana'

A very large flowered variety with lavender blue, rose tinted flowers with long, pointed sepals and brown stamens, produced from June to Sept. Suitable for East, South or West aspect. Best position has roots in shade, top in sun. Pruning optional, but best results if not pruned.

Clematis 'Madame Baron Veillard'

An attractive variety with lilac rose flowers. Suitable for East, South or West aspect. Best position has roots in shade, top in sun.

Clematis 'Miss Bateman'

A very free flowering hybrid with creamy white flowers 4 to 6 ins diameter with prominent chocolate-red stamens. There is a green bar down the centre of the petals when the flower first opens. Suitable for any aspect and requiring no regular pruning, a very useful clematis for the garden. A cool root run is essential.

Clematis 'Marie Boisselot' (syn.'Madame le Coultre').

A vigorous, free flowering variety with large, pure white flowers with yellow stamens and overlapping petals, produced from July to Sept. Suitable for any aspect. When grown in sun it is best to shade the roots. Pruning optional but best if not.

Clematis 'Mrs Cholmondeley'

A very large flowered variety with lavender blue flowers with long pointed sepals and brown stamens, produced from May to Sept. Suitable for any aspect. When grown in sun it is best to shade the roots. No regular pruning required.

Clematis 'Mrs N.Thompson'

A large flowered and very striking hybrid Clematis. Deep violet blooms with a vivid scarlet bar and deep red stamens. Suitable for any aspect except North facing. Flowers in May/June and again in September on the new growth. Very free flowering.

Clematis 'Nelly Moser'

One of the most popular clematis. Large, pale mauve pink flowers with deep carmine bars appear in May, June and Sept. No regular pruning needed. Flower colour best in shade or semi shade.

Clematis 'Ramona' (syn. hybrida Sieboldii)

A large flowered hybrid with lavender blue flowers with dark stamens from June to Sept. Suitable for any aspect. When planted in sun it is best to shade the roots. Pruning optional, but best results if not.

Clematis 'Rouge Cardinal'

An attractive variety with glowing crimson flowers and brown stamens, produced from June to Sept. Considered the best of the red clematis. Suitable for East, South or West aspect. Best position has roots in shade, top in sun.

Clematis 'Sealand Gem'

A very versatile and easy to please variety, pruning is optional and it is tolerant of sun and shade. Beautiful flowers 4' to 6' across of rosy-mauve with a pink bar down each petal. It has brown stamens.

Clematis 'The President'

A large flowered variety with handsome, deep purple flowers with reddish brown stamens, appearing from June to Sept. Suitable for any aspect. When grown in sun it is best to shade the roots. No regular pruning needed.

Clematis 'Ville de Lyon'

A very attractive variety with carmine red flowers, shading to deep crimson round the edge of the petals, with golden stamens at the centre. Freely produced from July to Oct. Suitable for East, South or West aspect. Best position has roots in shade, top in sun.

Clematis 'Voluceau'

A vigorous, free flowering hybrid with petunia red petals and yellow stamens from June to Sept. Suitable for East, South and West aspect. Best position has roots in shade, top in sun.

Clematis 'Vyvyan Pennell'

A beautiful and unusual variety. Double, violet blue flowers, shaded crimson, with golden stamens are produced in May and June, single flowers in September. Suitable for East, South or West facing aspect. Best position has roots in shade, top in sun. No pruning needed.

Clematis 'William Kennett'

A handsome variety with deep lavender flowers and dark purple stamens, appearing from June to Sept. Suitable for any aspect. When grown in sun it is best to shade the roots. Pruning optional but best results if not pruned.

Clematis alpina

A very beautiful clematis for the small garden with nodding flowers of satiny blue with whitish petaloid stamens. Does best in a cool or North facing aspect. Very free flowering and growing to a height of 6 to 8ft.

Clematis armandii

A very handsome evergreen clematis,first introduced in 1900 from china by Messrs Veitch, with large leathery three lobed leaves. The clusters of waxy white flowers about 2 ins across are sweetly scented and borne in profusion in March/April. Not reliably hardy and must be planted on a south or west facing wall.

Clematis flammula

A strong growing climber, forming a dense tangle of glabrous stems with bright green, bi-pinnate leaves. From August to October the plant is covered with loose panicles of small white, scented flowers, followed by silky seed heads.

Clematis macropetala

A delightful species Clematis with violet flowers, having conspicuous petaloide giving the affect of doubling. Fluffy, grey, silky seed heads follow similar to 'Old Man's Beard' of our hedgerow. The leaves are much divided and add to the plants charm. A native of China and Siberia and happy growing in any aspect including facing north.

Clematis macropetala 'Markham's Pink'

A lovely clematis, the nodding, double lavender pink flowers appear in April/May and have greenish white stamens. Suitable for any aspect, no pruning needed.

Clematis montana

One of the easiest flowering climbers to grow. Clusters of pure white flowers appear in May. Ideal for covering north facing walls, trees, outbuildings etc. Any aspect is suitable. When planted in sun it is best to shade the roots. No regular pruning needed.

Clematis montana 'Elizabeth'

A beautiful, small flowered variety, producing masses of soft pink flowers with yellow stamens in May and June. Very sweetly scented. Ideal for covering North facing walls or trees. Suitable for any aspect. When planted in sun it is best to shade the roots. No regular pruning needed.

Clematis montana 'Grandiflora'

A fast growing variety, producing masses of pure white flowers with yellow stamens in May and June. Ideal for covering North facing walls, trees or buildings. Suitable for any aspect. When planted in sun it is best to shade the roots. No regular pruning needed.

Clematis montana 'Tetrarose'

The largest flower in the montana group: 2-3 inches across, lilac rose with straw coloured stamens appearing in May and June. Attractive bronzy foliage. Suitable for any aspect. Ideal for covering north facing walls or trees. When planted in sun it is best to shade the roots. No regular pruning needed.

Clematis montana rubens

A vigorous, very free flowering variety with deep pink flowers and golden stamens in May and June. Attractive bronzy foliage. Ideal for covering North facing walls, trees or buildings. Suitable for any aspect. When planted in sun it is best to shade the roots. No regular pruning needed.

Clematis montana wilsonii

The last of the 'montana' group to flower, producing a mass of strongly scented 1-2ins flowers which open greenish white and mature to creamy white with a prominent boss of yellow stamens. The sepals are attractively twisted and the young shoots downy. Introduced by Wilson from Central China. When mature, a magnificant sight in June/July when covered in thousands of blooms.

Clematis spooneri

A clematis of the 'montana' group and should correctly be C. chrysocoma var. sericea. A vigorous climber up to 30 ft. with 2 inch pure white flowers with yellow stamens. The young stems and leaves are covered in a dense brownish yellow down. A good alternative to C. montana for covering unsightly walls or buildings.

Clematis tangutica

A delightful clematis with rich yellow, nodding flower heads followed by fluffy seed heads which are good for winter arrangements. Very easily grown and ideal for covering low walls, trellises, fences and banks. No regular pruning needed.

Clematis x durandii

A smaller flowered type with rich, indigo blue flowers with off white stamens, produced from June to Sept. Suitable for East, South and West aspect. Best position has roots in shade, top in sun. Semi herbaceous type, needs tying to support.

Eccremocarpus scaber

A vigorous climbing plant that requires a sheltered position. 1' long, tubular, orange scarlet flowers appear freely from June to October. It is often cut back to ground level by frost during the winter, but will quickly cover walls, fences etc. in one season.

Hedera canariensis 'Variegata'

A strikingly attractive evergreen climber. The quite large leaves are marked with green, grey and creamy white. Excellent for trellis work and low walls. Can also be used as a houseplant. May be cut back by frost in severe winters.

Hedera colchica 'Dentata Variegata'

A very ornamental, hardy ivy with large leaves, bright green shading to grey, edged creamy yellow when young, creamy white when mature. Self clinging to walls, tree stumps or as ground cover. Can be grown in tubs and troughs. Best colour in sun.

Hedera colchica 'Paddy's Pride' (Sulphur Heart)

An impressive variegated ivy with large leaves boldly marked with an irregular central splash of yellow, merging to pale then deep green. Self clinging to walls, tree stumps or as ground cover. Can be grown in tubs and troughs.

Hedera helix 'Anna Marie'

An evergreen climbing plant with small, attractive leaves edged with creamy white. Good for tubs, hanging baskets and ground cover as well as trellis and walls.

Hedera helix 'Boskoop'

An attractive small leaved form of ivy with green, pale veined leaves, many of them crimped, waved and folded. Good for climbing up walls, trees etc. and planting in tubs, also a very good evergreen ground cover plant.

Hedera helix 'Cavendishii'

A very pretty form of ivy. The leaves are variegated with green, grey and yellow, giving an unusual mottled effect. As this is one of the smaller leafed types, it can be used for tubs and troughs, as well as for ground cover, growing on walls and trees etc.

Hedera helix 'Cristata'

A distinct and unusual ivy with pale green, often rounded leaves which are attractively waved and crimped at the edges. Self clinging to walls, tree stumps or as ground cover. Can be grown in tubs and troughs.

Hedera helix 'Gavotte'

A fairly small leaved ivy with smooth, shiny heart shaped leaves. A good plant for growing up walls and fences etc. or as ground cover for tubs or troughs.

Hedera helix 'Glacier'

An evergreen climber with fairly small, green, grey and white leaves. This ivy can be grown as a houseplant as well as outside, and is good for hanging baskets and tubs.

Hedera helix 'Goldheart'

A strikingly attractive ivy with small, neat green leaves, each with a central splash of golden yellow, often tinges pink in winter. Self clinging to walls, tree stumps or as ground cover. Can be grown in tubs, troughs or hanging baskets.

Hedera helix 'Green Ripple'

An attractive climbing ivy. The jagged edged leaves have prominant lighter green veins which, when massed give a cascading effect.

Hedera helix 'Ivalace'

An unusual looking ivy with small, delicate leaves with rolled in edges. The foliage is shiny and deep green, lasting all year. A very attractive climber that will double as a ground cover plant if desired.

Hedera helix 'Little Picture'

A small leaved ivy with the leaves giving an overall frilly effect. Can be used to cover walls, fences, climbing up stumps etc. Is also a good ground cover plant for sun or shade.

Hedera helix 'Lutzii'

A useful evergreen climber that may also be used for ground cover. The leaves are mottled grey green with splashes of yellow and green. Good for sun or shade giving year round colour. Can cover stumps, walls and fences, be used in tubs, hanging baskets and even as a houseplant.

Hydrangea petiolaris

A strong growing, self clinging climber with green leaves and heads of white flowers in June and July. Very good for a north or north east facing wall or as a screening plant. Can also be grown as a shrub.

Jasminum officinale

A strong growing climber bearing pure white, deliciously fragrant flowers in clusters from June to Sept. Excellent for training against fences, or twining around arbours, trellises and pergolas.

Lonicera 'Dropmore Scarlet'

A beautiful, tall growing climber with clusters of tubular, bright orange scarlet, fragrant flowers, produced from July to October.

Lonicera (general)

This includes honeysuckles which are both evergreen or deciduous. They are rapid growing climbers and mostly bear fragrant flowers. The old wood needs to be cut out from time to time to keep them neat and in bounds.

Lonicera henryi

A vigorous, evergreen or semi evergreen with downy shoots and yellow flowers stained red in June and July followed by black berries. Can be used to cover other bushes, tree stumps, trellises and pergolas. Also as ground cover.

Lonicera japonica 'Aureo-reticulata'

A very useful carpeting evergreen, which thrives in shady conditions. Greenish white flowers appear in February andA vigorous, very free flowering variety with deep pink flowers and golden stamens in May and June. Attractive bronzy foliage

Lonicera japonica 'Halliana'

A vigorous, evergreen or semi evergreen honeysuckle with very fragrant flowers that open white, changing to yellow, appearing from June to Oct. Can be used to cover other bushes, tree stumps, trellises and pergolas. Also as ground cover.

Lonicera japonica var.repens (L.flexuosa)

A vigorous evergreen or semi evergreen climber, the leaves and shoots are flushed purple. The flowers are very fragrant, cream flushed purple, produced from June to October. Can be used to cover other bushes, tree stumps, trellises and pergolas. Also as ground cover.

Lonicera periclymenum 'Belgica'

A vigorous, bushy climber producing fragrant, reddish purple and yellow flowers in May and June, often again in late summer, followed by bright red berries. Can be used to cover other bushes, tree stumps, trellises and pergolas. Also as ground cover.

Lonicera periclymenum 'Serotina'

A vigorous, bushy climber, later flowering than L. 'Belgica', with flowers, rich reddish purple outside and creamy whiteiage. Ideal for covering North facing walls, trees or buildings. Suitable for any aspect. When planted in sun it is best to shade the roots. No regular pruning needed.

Lonicera x americana

A lovely variety of Honeysuckle with flowers 2' long, white passing to pale and finally deep yellow, heavily tinged purple outside. Provides a spectacular floral display in late June and July.

Lonicera x heckrottii 'Gold Flame'

A semi climbing species with fragrant, brilliant orange flowers, golden within, appearing from July to Sept.

Lonicera x tellmanniana

One of the most beautiful honeysuckles but unfortunately with out scent. The large flowers of deep golden yellow are flushed bronzy red at the tips and held in bunches of six to twelve. The overall effect from a distance is of vermilion-orange, the colour being more intense in in shade.

Parthenocissus henryana

A beautiful, self clinging vine, with dark green or bronze leaves with a silvery white line down every 'finger' of each leaf. In autumn the green turns brilliant red. Leaf colour best in partial shade. Good for growing up walls.

Parthenocissus quinquefolia

A vigorous, self clinging creeper with green leaves that turn brilliant shades of orange and scarlet in autumn. Good for growing on trees, walls and fences.

Parthenocissus tricuspidata 'Veitchii'

Often mistakenly called Virginia Creeper, this vine does not grow as large and has smaller, three lobed leaves. Superb autumn colours. Self clinging though may need initial support. Good for growing on trees, walls and fences.

Passiflora caerulea

A beautiful climbing plant with well known and indescribable flowers which are said to represent the Crucifixion. The base of the plant needs protection with peat or leaves for the first couple of winters till it is established. Suitable for training up strings, wires or trellis.

Pileostegia viburnoides

An evergreen climbing plant closely related to Hydrangeas, with clusters of white flowers in september and october. The plant clings to walls by means of aerial roots and will reach up to 20 feet in due course, densely covered with dullish green, strongly veined leaves. Will succeed in any aspect including shady or north facing. Award of Merit 1914.

Polygonum baldschuanicum

A very vigorous, showy climber with pale green, heart shaped leaves. Clusters of small white, pink tinged flowers appear in masses from July to Sept. Very good for screening, twining over old trees and on trellises or wires. Good fast growing ground cover.

Schizophragma hydrangeoides

A superb, unusual climber with hairy leaves and very large, flat flower heads, consisting of tiny white flowers surrounded by a ring of pale yellow bracts, freely produced in July and August. Self clinging with aerial roots. Good for walls, pergolas, or tree stumps.

Solanum crispum 'Glasnevin'

A quick growing, scrambling wall shrub. Very lovely in its cultivar 'Glasnevin' with masses of purple, slightly fragrant flowers with a cone of yellow anthers. Should be grown on a South or South West facing wall and does well on chalky soil. A relative of the potato and aubergine, this cultivar originated in the Glasnevin Botanical Garden, Dublin and is said to be hardier than the type.

Solanum jasminoides 'Album'

A fast growing, semi evergreen climbing plant that requires a sheltered wall or fence. Clusters of white, star shaped flowers with yellow centres appear from July to October. Remove weak growths in spring.

Trachelospermum jasminoides

A evergreen twining plant which needs the protection of a south or southwest wall. The jasmine-like flowers are very fragrant. Worth growing in a conservatory if no suitable spot is available outside.

Vitis 'Brant' (vinifera 'Brandt')

An excellent, dual purpose, hardy climbing plant, that has a crop of edible black grapes and magnificent autumn colour. If the crop is required for wine making, then proper pruning and feeding is necessary. Can be grown up a tree, old hedge or stump. May also be trained over walls, pergolas or fences.

Vitis coignetiae

A spectacular climbing vine of vigorous growth. The rounded, mid green leaves have rust red hairs beneath. In autumn they turn glorious shades of yellow, orange-red and purple-crimson. Green flowers are followed by inedible black berries with a purple bloom. Very effective when grown up a tree, old hedge or stump. May also be trained over walls, pergolas or fences.

Wisteria floribunda 'Macrobotrys'

A superb climber with leaves composed of thirteen to nineteen ovate, dark green leaflets. Massive racemes of fragrant, lilac tinged flowers appear in May.

Wisteria floribunda 'Peaches and Cream'

The flowers are flushed rosy-pink in bud opening to almost white. Racemes 15 inches long. Attractive light green, pinnate leaves.

Wisteria floribunda 'Purple Patches'

Long racemes of violet-purple flowers. Attractive light green, pinnate leaves.

Wisteria floribunda 'Rosea'

A superb variety of Wisteria with very long racemes of pale rose, purple tipped flowers up to three feet long. The stems twine anti clockwise as against the Chinese Wisteria which twines clockwise.

Wisteria sinensis

One of the noblest of climbers, with 8-12 inch long racemes of fragrant, mauve flowers in May and June. Use against walls, trees and pergolas. Initial support needed when grown against walls or fences.

Wisteria sinensis 'Pink Ice' (Honbeni)

A slightly later flowering form of wisteria. Dark rosy pink bunches of flowers appear in May, June. This is a grafted plant not a seedling, which means that it will flower much earlier in its life. If grown on a chalky soil add plenty of loam.

Wisteria sinensis 'Reindeer' (Jakoh Fuji)

A white flowered form of wisteria with beautifully fragrant, foot long tassels of flowers in May, June. This is a grafted plant not a seedling, which means that it will flower much earlier in its life. If grown on a chalky soil add plenty of loam.

CLIMBERS

BOTANICAL NAME	COMMON NAME
Actinidia chinensis	– Chinese Gooseberry
Actinidia kolomikta	– Kolomikta Vine
Campsis	– Trumpet Vine
Clematis alpina	– Alpine Clematis
Clematis flammula	– Fragrant Virgin's Bower
Eccremocarpus scaber	– Chilean Glory Flower
Hedera Helix 'Hibernica'	– Irish Ivy
Hedera canariensis 'Variegata'	– Gloire de Marengo, Marengo Ivy
Hedera colchica 'Dentata Variegata'	– Variegated Persian Ivy
Hedera colchica	– Ivy
Hydrangea petiolaris	– Japanese Climbing Hydrangea
Jasminum officinale	– White Jasmine
Lonicera	– Honeysuckle
Lonicera periclymenum 'Belgica'	– Early Dutch Honeysuckle
Lonicera periclymenum 'Serotina'	– Late Dutch Honeysuckle
Parthenocissus henryana	– Chinese Virginia Creeper
Parthenocissus quinquefolia	– Virginia Creeper
Parthenocissus tricuspidata 'Veitchii'	– Boston Ivy
Passiflora caerulea	– Passion Flower
Polygonum baldschuanicum	– Russian Vine
Solanum jasminoides 'Album'	– Jasmine Nightshade
Vitis coignetiae	– Japanese Crimson Glory Vine
Wisteria floribunda	– Japanese Wisteria
Wisteria sinensis	– Chinese Wisteria

CLIMBERS

COMMON NAME	BOTANICAL NAME
Alpine Clematis	– Clematis alpina
Boston Ivy	– Parthenocissus tricuspidata 'Veitchii'
Chilean Glory Flower	– Eccremocarpus scaber
Chinese Gooseberry	– Actinidia chinensis
Chinese Virginia Creeper	– Parthenocissus henryana
Chinese Wisteria	– Wisteria sinensis
Climbing Hydrangea	– Hydrangea petiolaris
Crimson Glory Vine	– Vitis coignetiae
Fragrant Virgin's Bower	– Clematis flammula
Honeysuckle	– Lonicera
Honeysuckle Early Dutch	– Lonicera periclymenum 'Belgica'
Honeysuckle Late Dutch	– Lonicera periclymenum 'Serotina'
Ivy	– Hedera
Japanese Wisteria	– Wisteria floribunda 'Macrobotrys'
Kolomikta Vine	– Actinidia kolomikta
Passion Flower	– Passiflora caerulea
Russian Vine	– Polygonum baldschuanicum
Trumpet Vine	– Campsis radicans
Virginia Creeper	– Parthenocissus quinquefolia
White Jasmine	– Jasminum officinale
Wisteria, Chinese	– Wisteria sinensis
Wisteria, Japanese	– Wisteria floribunda